United States
Military Medals
and Ribbons

United States Military Medals and Ribbons

by PHILIP K. ROBLES

Charles E. Tuttle Company
RUTLAND·VERMONT TOKYO·JAPAN

Representatives

CONTINENTAL EUROPE:
Boxerbooks, Inc., Zurich
BRITISH ISLES:
Prentice-Hall International, Inc., London
AUSTRALASIA:
Paul Flesch & Co., Pty. Ltd., Melbourne
CANADA:
M. G. Hurtig, Ltd., Edmonton

Published by the Charles E. Tuttle Company, Inc.
of Rutland, Vermont & Tokyo, Japan, with editorial
offices at Suido 1-chome, 2-6, Bunkyo-ku, Tokyo

Copyright in Japan, 1971
by Charles E. Tuttle Company, Inc.
All rights reserved

Library of Congress Catalog Card No. 75-147178
International Standard Book No. 0-8048-0048-0

First printing, 1971
Third printing, 1973

Layout of plates by Hide Doki
PRINTED IN JAPAN

TABLE OF CONTENTS

LIST OF ILLUSTRATIONS

PREFACE

This book was originally begun as a consolidation of the awards and decorations regulations of the United States Armed Forces, compiled simply to aid me in my work as a Personal Affairs Technician in the United States Air Force.

A large number of Air Force personnel have served in the other services, and questions keep occurring about their ribbons and the authority to wear them. To make my job easier, I acquired, with considerable difficulty, copies of the regulations of the Army, Navy, Marine Corps, and Coast Guard, and proceeded to consolidate the mass. Shortly I was enmeshed in a web of cross-references to other regulations, laws, statutes, latitudes, longitudes, executive orders, and other data which I know to be essential in regulations, but, nevertheless, a confusing array of trivia to one who is neither a lawyer nor a geographer.

Eliminating the extraneous verbiage from the regulations soon proved to be a formidable task, but the end result has enabled me to answer most of the questions concerning eligibility for award and wear of the medals of the United States Armed Forces. This search for data led me into a fascinating hobby and avocation. Delving deeper into the subject, I found that there were few authoritative books available for reference which would be of interest to both the professional military man and to the civilian. This volume is the result of my efforts.

Much generalization has been necessary in describing the criteria for these medals, but all data regarding periods of eligibility and specific service requirements have been extracted directly from regulations current as of the date of this writing.

In many cases it will be observed that the authority for some Air Force decorations and medals is the same as for Army awards. The reason for this is because prior to 18 September 1947, the Air Force (then the Army Air Corps) was part of the Army, and, in a sense, the Army can be called the parent of the Air Force. A part of the transfer act in 1947 provided for the continued award of Army decorations to Air Force personnel under the original authorities. Later, amendments to the original authorities provided for the establishment of distinctive Air Force awards. Although the Air Force became a separate, autonomous service in 1947, it was not until 1957 that it began creating its own distinctive decorations.

After some hesitation, I decided to add Merchant Marine awards to this collection, although they are the awards of a civilian agency. I did so because the various services generally allow military personnel who earned these awards while serving in the Merchant Marine to wear them on their military uniforms. Too, during World War II, the officers and men of the Merchant Marine were exposed to the same risks as our service personnel, died as readily, and many of them spent years as prisoners of war. They were under essentially the same discipline as military personnel and, during World War II, wore uniforms almost indistinguishable from those of the United States Navy.

To make this book as complete as possible, I have tried to provide the name of the designer of each medal. However, it has not been possible to do so because the awards branches of the various military departments do not have the information. In many instances medal designs were the result of a group effort, amended or modified at various command levels, with no one individual being singled out as the designer.

My thanks go to the many people who have helped me in this effort and especially to Satoya Tobin and William Smith of Fussa-shi, Japan, and Peter Brogren.

Philip K. Robles
TECHNICAL SERGEANT
USAF

INTRODUCTION

Throughout history men have been awarded tokens of esteem and respect for outstanding deeds in time of peace and war. In the military these tokens have usually been bits of ribbon, medals, badges, sashes, etc., to be worn on the individual's uniform.

Late in the 17th century various countries instituted the custom of issuing medals to all participants in a particular campaign or battle. It was not until the 19th century, however, that the custom really took hold. Since then every country that has engaged in wars or other strife has issued medals to commemorate participation in battles or campaigns. Invariably each nation produced one or more campaign medals. Since World War II, the United States alone has created 60 decorations and campaign medals to say nothing of the limitless new insignia, uniforms, and qualification badges occasioned by new war machines and techniques. As a result, very few people can readily recognize all the ribbons worn by servicemen today, and I would not hesitate to say that even fewer know the criteria for awarding most ribbons.

Unlike most countries, the United States government is not addicted to creating and issuing a great number of civil awards for each and every achievement of its citizens. Those few awards established for civilians are not discussed here because the primary purpose of this book is to cover those of the military establishment.

The United States military establishment has no orders, i.e., an award conferred by the head of state which is often restricted to "blooded" or "titled" citizens, and is further restricted in its number of members.

Decorations are awards to recognize heroism, meritorious

or outstanding service, or achievement. Service and campaign medals are awards to recognize participation in a certain battle or service during a specific period, or in a particular area. Appurtenances and devices are small metal emblems clasped to ribbons to indicate participation in a battle, further qualification on the basic award, or to denote additional awards of a medal.

Normally, the individual who possesses awards has the option of wearing them if he chooses. The exceptions: his superior officer may prescribe that they be worn with specific uniforms; they may not be worn with fatigues (coveralls, dungarees); nor may they be worn while undergoing confinement in a military facility. Anyone, civilian or military, discovered wearing medals and decorations to which he is not entitled is liable to severe punishment and possible imprisonment under various federal laws.

In time of peace servicemen may not unconditionally accept decorations from foreign governments. This ruling has its origin in our *Constitution*, which prohibits U.S. citizens from ". . . accepting any present, emolument, office, or title of any kind whatsoever from any king, prince, or foreign state" (Article I, Section 9). A serviceman may accept the decoration when it is presented to him, but he must thereafter submit the decoration and all pertinent data to the military department of which he is a member. Only after the approval of the serviceman's departmental secretary may he wear the medal on his uniform. Foreign decorations received during peacetime may be worn only after Congress has authorized their wear. During periods of war or national emergency, Congress has given a blanket authority for American servicemen to accept awards tendered by cobelligerent nations; however, career members are normally authorized to accept decorations only after they retire from the service.

Foreign decorations and awards earned while serving in the armed forces of another nation, which was a neutral or cobelligerent with the United States in World War II, may be worn on the uniform if permission is obtained from the appropriate departmental secretary. In addition, ribbons earned subsequent to World War II by individuals serving in the armed forces of another nation may be worn. However, at least one U.S. decoration or award must be worn when foreign awards are displayed.

United States
Military Medals
and Ribbons

1

U.S. MILITARY DECORATIONS

United States military decorations were first established and authorized by Gen. George Washington on 7 August 1782, when he ordered a heart-shaped badge of purple cloth edged with a narrow lace or binding to be given to officers and men alike who displayed unusual gallantry or extraordinary fidelity and essential service. The award was named the Badge of Military Merit (p. 57), and was designed by Charles L'Enfant. Only three were known to have been issued and the badge fell into disuse after the Revolutionary War. Other medals were issued during that war, antedating the Badge of Military Merit, but since these were specially struck medals intended only for specific individuals and feats, they do not properly fall into the category discussed here. It is interesting to note that General Washington, in establishing the Badge of Military Merit, provided for its award to officers and men alike and, in concluding his order, stated: "The road to glory in a patriot army and a free country is thus opened to all."

Twenty years later on 19 May 1802, Napoleon Bonaparte established the Legion d'Honneur, which, like the Badge of Military Merit, provided for award to persons other than officers. The Legion d'Honneur has been credited as being the mainstay of Napoleon's systems of reward and also credited with a major part of the splendid *esprit de corps* and loyalty he enjoyed from his troops. His use of the Legion d'Honneur as an award to all persons regardless of their position was masterful, and today, more than a century and a half later, the award is still in force and is highly coveted.

Although the Badge of Military Merit did not find such ready and widespread adoption during the Revolutionary War, on 22 February 1932, the 200th anniversary of George

Washington's birth, Gen. Douglas MacArthur, then Chief of Staff, United States Army, directed in War Department General Order No. 3 that the badge be ". . . revived out of respect to his [General Washington] memory and military achievements." Redesignated simply as the "Purple Heart" (p. 57), the first military decoration made available by any nation to fighting men of all ranks continues as a cherished token of the respect and esteem in which the father of his country is held.

There are 28 United States military decorations currently authorized for award to U.S. Armed Forces. They are included here, and in addition, two medals awarded by the Treasury Department are included. Even though the latter are not primarily military decorations, the language of their establishment is such that it does not preclude their award and wear by members of the armed services.

There are, of course, more U.S. military decorations but their award was made so long ago that the recipients are no longer on active duty, and in many cases are deceased. These awards, made obsolete by the passage of time, have not lost the luster of their glory and are covered in a separate section.

Decorations differ from service and campaign medals in that they are usually of a distinct shape, i.e., a star, cross, etc., while service and campaign medals are always disk shaped. Too, a decoration is awarded for an outstanding act or service of a specific individual and is a reward for meritorious service, outstanding achievement, or an act of gallantry. For award, some require outstanding performance of duty; others require acts of heroism involving the voluntary risk of life. Whatever the decoration and its criteria for award, the individual who is the recipient is truly a person of note.

MEDAL OF HONOR

The Medal of Honor is the highest-ranked and best-known U.S. decoration. It compares in prestige and precedence to the British Victoria Cross. Often mistitled the "Congressional Medal of Honor," it is in fact awarded in the name of the Congress of the United States and, whenever possible, the President of the United States personally makes its presentation.

U.S. Air Force and U.S. Army regulations, which are based on an Act of Congress of 9 July 1918, provide for the award when ". . . any person who while in the military service of the United States distinguishes himself conspicuously by gallantry and intrepidity at the risk of his life, above and beyond the call of duty . . . involving conspicuous risk of life, the omission of which could not justly cause censure." U.S. Navy, U.S. Marine Corps, and U.S. Coast Guard regulations, which are based on an Act of Congress of 7 August 1942, contain the same wording but also include an additional qualifying criterion which allows for the award to a person who ". . . in the line of his profession, distinguishes . . ."

Only a few times in recent history has the Medal of Honor been awarded under conditions other than those prescribed by the existing statutes. Among these have been the awards made to Brig. Gen. (then Captain) Charles A. Lindbergh, U.S. Air Force Reserve, for his historic New York–Paris flight on 20 and 21 May 1927; to Adm. (then Commander) Richard E. Byrd and to Floyd G. Bennett for their North Pole flight on 9 May 1926. Some quarters have expressed surprise and regret that America's astronaut, Lt. Col. John Glenn, was not awarded the Medal of Honor for his momentous orbit of the earth instead of the little-known National Space Agency Distinguished Service Medal. However, since the space orbit of the earth was not intended for military purposes, the Medal of Honor might have been inappropriate.

There are currently three designs of the Medal of Honor, two issued by the Air Force and Army, respectively, the other by the Navy, Marine Corps, and Coast Guard. The present medals have evolved from the original designs as a result of legislative actions, for aesthetic reasons, and to render useless the many imitations issued by patriotic societies.

Sen. James W. Grimes of Iowa first proposed in 1861 that a medal of honor be provided for enlisted men of the Navy; however, his proposal was strongly opposed by the Senate Military Committee. The opposition was based on this young nation's abhorrence of the titles, orders, etc., of European monarchies of which it had rid itself by its *Declaration of Independence* from Great Britain. Nevertheless, the measure did pass the houses of Congress and was approved by President Lincoln on 21 December 1861. Shortly thereafter, on 12 July 1862, the President approved another bill which provided for medals of honor for enlisted men of the Army and volunteer forces. Still later, additional bills were passed extending eligibility for the award to commissioned officers.

Although the original intent of the Navy and Army bills had been to reward men for distinguishing themselves by gallantry in action and for seamanlike and soldierlike conduct, a lack of specific criteria and restrictions on the award soon led to widespread abuses. For the first few decades after its inception there was no consistent policy on criteria for the medal's award, nor were there any clear-cut rules for the documentation and validation of feats befitting this award.

Finally, in 1916, after much urging from public-spirited citizens and the Legion of the Medal of Honor Organization, Congress passed legislation which provided for, among other things, the establishment of a board to investigate and report upon past awards of the Army Medal of Honor. This board gathered all the records of Medals of Honor awarded up to 16 October 1916, and reviewed them. Of the 2,625 medals that had been awarded, the board struck 911 from the list; 864 awards had been made to one regiment. On 9 July 1918, Congress redefined the criteria and set forth clear-cut rules for the award. Thus the prestige of the Medal of Honor was affirmed and has so continued to date.

Since 1918 there have been few amendments to the acts relating to the Medal of Honor; the latest amendment, and perhaps the most important, provides for a $100-a-month pension to holders of the medal who make application for it. A privilege extended to Medal of Honor winners whether they are on active or inactive duty is space-available transportation via military aircraft within the continental limits of the United States. Another privilege that is not so widely known provides for the sons of Medal of Honor winners to be admitted to United States military academies without regard to regional quotas, provided they are otherwise qualified.

A common belief held by servicemen and veterans is that one should salute Medal of Honor winners regardless of grade or rank. This is not stipulated in regulations, but the professional military man certainly would have no compunctions about honoring a holder of the Medal of Honor.

The Medal of Honor is the only "neck" decoration awarded by the armed forces to U.S. military personnel. When in a uniform calling for service ribbons only, it is worn on a ribbon bar along with other ribbons; in ceremonial or formal dress it is worn around the neck. In civilian attire, a white-starred blue rosette may be worn in the lapel. No miniature device is authorized for the Medal of Honor.

AIR FORCE

Plate 1 Designed by the Institute of Heraldry, U.S. Army, the Air
(p. 33) Force Medal of Honor is a gold-finished five-pointed bronze
star (one point down) 2″ in diameter, with rays terminating
in trefoils on a wreath of laurel in green enamel. Each ray of
the star contains a crown of laurel and oak on a green enamel
background; in the center is a representation of the head of
the Statue of Liberty surrounded by an amulet of 34 stars
(the number of states in 1862). The star is suspended by rings
from a trophy consisting of a bar inscribed with the word
"VALOR" above an adaption of the thunderbolt from the
USAF coat of arms.

The bar is suspended from a light blue silk-*moiré* neckband
$1\frac{3}{16}$″ wide and $21\frac{3}{4}$″ long behind a square pad in the center
made of the ribbon with in-turned corners, and charged with
13 white stars in the form of a triple chevron.

Air Force Manual 900-3 is the directive covering this award;
authorized by Act of Congress, 9 July 1918, and awarded pursuant to Section 8741, Title 10 USC (United States Code).

ARMY

Plate 2 Designed by Maj. Gen. George L. Gillespie in 1904, the Army
(p. 33) Medal of Honor is a gold-finished five-pointed star (one point
down) $1\frac{9}{16}$″ in diameter, with rays terminating in trefoils on a
laurel wreath in green enamel. Each ray of the star contains an
oak leaf in green enamel; in the center is the head of Minerva
surrounded by the inscription "UNITED STATES OF AMERICA."
The star is suspended by two links from a bar bearing the
inscription "VALOR" and surmounted by an eagle grasping
laurel leaves in one talon and arrows in the other. On the
reverse of the bar is inscribed "THE CONGRESS TO."

The bar is suspended by a hook to a ring fastened behind
the eagle, and the hook is attached to a light blue silk-*moiré*
neckband $1\frac{3}{16}$″ wide and $21\frac{3}{4}$″ long behind a square pad in
the center made of the ribbon with in-turned corners, and
charged with 13 white stars in the form of a triple chevron.

Army Regulation 672-5-1 is the directive covering this
award authorized by Act of Congress, 23 April 1904; 9 July
1918 (40 Stat. 870); Section 1403, Title 10 USC; ML1949,
Section 903. (Original authority for creation of the award
was a Resolution of Congress, 12 July 1862.)

NAVY, MARINE CORPS, AND COAST GUARD

Plate 3
(p. 34)
Designed by Christian Schussel and sculpted by Anthony C. Paquet in 1861, the Navy Medal of Honor is a $2\frac{1}{8}''$ diameter five-pointed bronze star (one point down), with rays terminating in trefoils. Each ray of the star contains a crown of laurel and oak; in the center is Minerva in conflict with a figure representing Discord in a circle of 34 stars. An anchor is attached to the top of the star. The ring of the anchor is suspended from a light blue silk-*moiré* neckband $1\frac{3}{16}''$ wide and $21\frac{3}{4}''$ long behind a square pad in the center made of the ribbon with in-turned corners, and charged with 13 white stars in the form of a triple chevron.

Navy Personnel Instructions P1650.1C is the directive covering this award; authorized by Act of Congress, 21 December 1861; 3 March 1901; 3 March 1915; 4 February 1919; and 7 August 1942. The 1942 act superseded all previous ones.

AIR FORCE CROSS

Plate 4
(p. 34)
The Air Force Cross is the second highest USAF decoration, ranking with the Army's Distinguished Service Cross and the Navy Cross. It is one of the first to be established as a unique Air Force award. Until its creation the Air Force had used the Army's DSC award. (The USAF was formed principally from the old Army Air Corps and continued to use decorations which, by the wording of the statutes, were established for the U.S. Army.)

The AFC may be awarded to ". . . any person who while serving in any capacity with the Air Force, distinguishes himself by extraordinary heroism in connection with military operations against an armed enemy of the United States. The act of heroism performed must involve risk of life so extraordinary as to set the person apart from his contemporaries." It may also be awarded to other members of the United States Armed Forces and to members of the armed forces of friendly nations who are so recommended.

Designed by Eleanor Cox, a former employee of the

Awards Division, Headquarters United States Air Force, the AFC is a $1\frac{5}{16}''$ bronze cross with an oxidized satin finish. In the center of the cross is a gold-plated American Bald Eagle, wings displayed against a cloud formation (from the Air Force crest) encircled by a laurel wreath in green enamel. The ribbon is Brittany Blue, edged with Old Glory Red, and bears a narrow white vertical stripe inside the red edges. Succeeding awards are denoted by bronze oak-leaf clusters. A miniature enameled metal lapel device may be worn when in civilian attire.

Air Force Manual 900-3 is the directive covering this award; authorized by Act of Congress, 6 July 1960, which amended Section 8742, Title 10 USC.

DISTINGUISHED SERVICE CROSS

Plate 5
(p. 34)

The Distinguished Service Cross is the second highest award of the Army, ranking with the Air Force Cross and the Navy Cross. Its award is usually made by the President through recommendations submitted by the Army.

The same Act of Congress which clarified the rules for the person who, after 6 April 1917, ". . . distinguishes himself by extraordinary heroism in connection with military operations against an armed enemy of the United States. The act of heroism performed must involve risk of life so extraordinary as to set the person apart from his contemporaries." It may also be awarded to other members of the United States Armed Forces and to members of the armed forces of friendly nations who are so recommended.

Designed by Capt. Aymar Embury, U.S. Army, the SCD is a bronze cross $2''$ high and $1\frac{13}{16}''$ wide. In the center of the cross is an American Bald Eagle and below the eagle is a scroll bearing the inscription "FOR VALOR." On the reverse, the center of the cross is circled with a wreath. The cross is suspended by a ring from a red, white, and blue ribbon similar to the AFC. Succeeding awards are denoted by bronze oak-leaf clusters. A miniature enameled metal lapel device may be worn when in civilian attire.

Army Regulation 672-5-1 is the directive covering this award; authorized by Act of Congress, 9 July 1918.

NAVY CROSS

Plate 6
(p. 35) The Navy Cross is the second highest award of the Navy, ranking with the Air Force Cross and the Army's Distinguished Service Cross. Between 1919 and 1942, the NC was awarded in noncombat as well as combat situations and ranked third rather than second in precedence of naval awards. Its award is usually made by the President through recommendations of the Navy.

The NC may be awarded to ". . . any person who while serving in any capacity with the Navy, distinguishes himself by extraordinary heroism in connection with military operations against an armed enemy of the United States. The act of heroism performed must involve risk of life so extraordinary as to set the person apart from his contemporaries." This criteria was established in 1942. The NC may also be awarded to other members of the United States Armed Forces and to members of the armed forces of friendly nations who are so recommended.

Designed by James E. Fraser, the NC is a rounded, dark bronze cross with a sailing vessel superimposed in a circle in the center of the cross. Wave scrolls are indicated under the vessel. On the reverse are crossed anchors and the initials "U.S.N." Succeeding awards are denoted by gold stars. A miniature enameled metal lapel device may be worn when in civilian attire. The pendant is about $1\frac{1}{2}''$ in diameter and the ribbon $1\frac{3}{8}''$ wide.

Navy Personnel Instructions P1650.1C is the directive covering this award; authorized by Act of Congress, 4 February 1919 and 7 August 1942.

DISTINGUISHED SERVICE MEDAL

The Distinguished Service Medal is the nation's highest award for distinguished service not involving personal bravery. It may be awarded to any person serving in any capacity of the United States Armed Forces who distinguishes himself by exceptionally meritorious service to the government in a duty of great responsibility. This responsibility has been defined as the exercise of authority or judgment in duties which decide the successful outcome of any major military operation. Civilians and foreign nationals are eligible for the award only under exceptional circumstances.

The Army DSM was established by the same legislation which provided for the Distinguished Service Cross. Between 1918 and 1934, awards of the Army DSM were made, upon application, to holders of the obsolete Certificate of Merit (page 133). Holders of the Certificate of Merit, after 1934, could have a Distinguished Service Cross substituted instead.

Individual designs of the Distinguished Service Medal are awarded by the Air Force, Army, Coast Guard, and Navy.

AIR FORCE

Plate 7
(p. 35)

Designed by the Air Force Heraldic Section, Institute of Heraldry, U.S. Army, the Air Force DSM, $2\frac{1}{4}''$ in diameter, is described: at the center of a sunburst of 13 gold rays separated by 13 white enamel stars is a blue stone representing the firmament. The ribbon is predominantly white and is banded in old gold, ultramarine, and smaller old gold stripes. Succeeding awards are denoted by bronze oak-leaf clusters.

Air Force Manual 900-3 is the directive covering this award; authorized by Act of Congress, 9 July 1918, and awarded pursuant to Section 8743, Title 10 USC.

ARMY

Plate 8
(p. 35)

Designed by Capt. Aymar Embury, U.S. Army, and sculpted by Corp. Gaetano Cecere, U.S. Army, the Army DSM is a $1\frac{1}{2}''$ inscribed circle of blue enamel containing the inscriptions "FOR DISTINGUISHED SERVICE" and "MCMXVIII" supporting the United States coat of arms. The ribbon is predominantly white and banded in red; the red is separated from the white by blue lines. Succeeding awards are denoted by bronze oak-leaf clusters.

Army Regulation 672-5-1 is the directive covering this award; authorized by Act of Congress, 9 July 1918, and awarded pursuant to Section 8743, Title 10 USC.

COAST GUARD

Plate 9
(p. 36) The Coast Guard DSM is a gold disk, suspended on a $1\frac{3}{8}''$ ribbon of grotto blue, white, and imperial purple. It bears the inscriptions "U.S. COAST GUARD" and "DISTINGUISHED SERVICE" in a circle around the traditional sailing vessel on wave scrolls. Succeeding awards are denoted by gold stars. Authority is 14 USC 492.

NAVY

Plate 10
(p. 36) Designed by Paul Manship, the Navy DSM is a quite heavy, circular, gilded bronze medal $1\frac{3}{8}''$ in diameter with what may be wave scrolls banding the entire edge. Within the scroll band is a circle of blue enamel containing the inscriptions "UNITED STATES OF AMERICA" and "NAVY" in gold lettering. In the center is the traditional eagle with opened wings gripping in its right talon an olive branch and in its left, arrows. The pendant is suspended by a white-enameled star on which is superimposed a gold anchor. The ribbon is predominantly navy blue with a narrow center stripe of gold. Succeeding awards are denoted by gold stars.

Navy Personnel Instructions P1650.1C is the directive covering this award; authorized by Act of Congress, 4 February 1919 and 7 August 1942.

SILVER STAR MEDAL

Plate 11
(p. 36) The Silver Star Medal may be awarded to any person—military, civilian, or foreign—who, while serving in any capacity with the United States Armed Forces, distinguishes himself by gallantry in action against an enemy of the United States; while engaged in military operations involving conflict with an opposing foreign force; or while serving with friendly foreign forces engaged in an armed conflict against an opposing armed force in which the United States is not a belligerent party. Gallantry in action means heroism of high degree involving risk of life.

The Silver Star had its origin in the 9 July 1918 Act of Congress which has played such a large role in American decorations. First authorized as a $\frac{3}{16}''$ citation star to be worn on the ribbon bar and suspension ribbon of appropriate campaign medals by Army personnel cited for gallantry in action, it was not until 1932 that the present design was created. On 7 August 1942 legislation was passed extending eligibility for the award to Navy personnel, thus making the SS the highest ranking, identically designed decoration that could be awarded by all the U.S. armed services.

Designed by Bailey, Banks and Biddle, a firm that was frequently utilized by the War and Navy departments for designing awards and decorations, the SS is simple in design but striking in appearance. It is a gold-colored star $1\frac{1}{2}''$ in circumscribing diameter on which in the center thereof is a $\frac{3}{16}''$ raised silver star, the center lines of all rays of both stars coinciding. The reverse bears the inscription "FOR GALLANTRY IN ACTION." The star is suspended by a rectangular-shaped metal loop with rounded corners from a silk-*moiré* ribbon having a center band of red flanked by equal bands of white; the white bands are flanked by equal blue bands having borders of white lines with blue edgings. Succeeding awards are denoted by bronze oak-leaf clusters for Air Force and Army awards and by gold stars for Navy, Marine Corps, and Coast Guard. A miniature enameled metal lapel device may be worn when in civilian attire.

Air Force Manual 900-3, Army Regulation 672-5-1, and Navy Personnel Instructions P1650.1C are the directives covering this award; authorized by Act of Congress, 9 July 1918 and 7 August 1942, and awarded pursuant to Section 8746, Title 10 USC.

LEGION OF MERIT

The Legion of Merit may be awarded to any member of the United States Armed Forces or foreign armed forces who distinguishes himself by exceptionally meritorious conduct in the performance of outstanding service to the United States.

The award is made to U.S. military personnel without degree; however, awards to members of foreign armed forces are made in the degrees of Chief Commander, Commander, Officer, and Legionnaire. The first two degrees are comparable in rank to awards of the Distinguished Service Medal to U.S. military personnel and are usually awarded to heads of state and to commanders of armed forces, respectively. The last two degrees are comparable in rank to the award of the Legion of Merit without degree to U.S. personnel.

The LOM was the first decoration to be designed with award to foreigners as its intent and also the first to have varying degrees. In the period immediately following its creation, the LOM was awarded in degrees to a few senior-ranking U.S. military officers, but the practice was quickly discontinued. It is not known whether the military services ever amended the orders awarding the higher degrees to Americans, but as recently as 1965, one command in the Air Force was found to be issuing the LOM in the degree of Officer to personnel who had been awarded the decoration in the degree of Legionnaire, as is customary for U.S. personnel. The rationale was that since these were officers being awarded the decoration, they should be presented with the Officer degree.

Designed by Col. Townsend Heard, U.S. Army, and sculpted by Katherine W. Lane, the LOM is as follows:

Chief Commander (1st degree)

Plate 12
(p. 37)
The Chief Commander degree is a domed, five-pointed American white star plaque of heraldic form bordered in purplish red enamel $2\frac{15}{16}''$ in circumscribing diameter with 13 white stars on a blue field emerging from a circle of clouds on the obverse. Backing the star is a laurel wreath with pierced, crossed arrows pointing outward between each arm of the star and the wreath. The reverse bears the inscription "UNITED STATES OF AMERICA."

Commander (2nd degree)

Plate 13
(p. 37)
The Commander degree is a five-pointed American white star plaque of heraldic form bordered in purplish red enamel $2\frac{1}{4}''$ in circumscribing diameter with 13 white stars on a blue field emerging from a circle of clouds. Backing the star is a laurel wreath with pierced, crossed arrows pointing outward between each arm of the star and the wreath. A bronze wreath connects an oval suspension ring to a neck ribbon. The reverse of the star isen ameled in white and bordered in purplish red enamel; in the center is a disk surrounded by the inscriptions "ANNUIT COEPTIS" and "MDCCLXXXII," and on the scroll

"UNITED STATES OF AMERICA." The silk-*moiré* ribbon is $21\frac{1}{4}''$ long and $1\frac{15}{16}''$ wide, composed of a bank of purplish red ($1\frac{13}{16}''$) with edges of white ($\frac{1}{16}''$).

Officer (3rd degree)

Plate 14
(p. 37)
The Officer degree is a five-pointed American white star of heraldic form bordered in purplish red enamel $1\frac{7}{8}''$ in circumscribing diameter with 13 white stars on a blue field emerging from a circle of clouds. Backing the star is a laurel wreath with modeled, crossed arrows pointing outward between each arm of the star and the wreath, and an all-bronze device of the same design as the pendant $\frac{3}{4}''$ in diameter on the center of the suspension ribbon. The reverse carries the same inscription as the Commander degree. The pendant is suspended by a silk-*moiré* ribbon $1\frac{7}{8}''$ long and $1\frac{3}{8}''$ wide, composed of a band of purplish red ($1\frac{1}{4}''$) with edges of white ($\frac{1}{16}''$).

Legionnaire (4th degree)

Plate 15
(p. 37)
The Legionnaire degree is identical to that of the Officer except the small bronze replica is not worn on the ribbon.

When wearing ribbons without the pendant or badge, a standard $1\frac{3}{8}''$ ribbon is worn with devices on the first three degrees. The device on the Chief Commander ribbon is a gold-colored miniature star in the shape of the medal, centered on a gold-colored bar. The Commander ribbon device is silver-colored and identical in design to that of the Chief Commander. The Officer device is a gold-colored miniature star without bar. Succeeding awards are denoted by bronze oak-leaf clusters for Air Force and Army awards and by gold stars for Navy, Marine Corps, and Coast Guard. In addition, the Navy, Marine Corps, and Coast Guard personnel wear a V device on the ribbon to show that the medal was earned in a combat situation. When the decoration is awarded more than once to a military member of a friendly foreign nation, subsequent awards are never made in a degree lower than the one originally awarded.

Air Force Manual 900-3, Army Regulation 672-5-1, and Navy Personnel Instructions P1650.1C are the directives covering this award; authorized by Act of Congress, 20 July 1942, and awarded pursuant to Section 1121, Title 10 USC.

DISTINGUISHED FLYING CROSS

Plate 16
(p. 38)
The Distinguished Flying Cross may be awarded to any person, who after 6 April 1917, while serving in any capacity with the United States Armed Forces, "distinguishes himself" while participating in aerial flight. Both heroism and achievement must be entirely distinctive, involving operations that are not routine. Combat service is not a requisite. The medal may also be awarded to members of the armed forces of friendly foreign nations who are serving with U.S. forces and, by special authority of Congress, to outstanding pioneers of aviation, regardless of status.

Designed by Elizabeth Will and Arthur E. DuBois, the DFC, a sharply defined and highly symbolic decoration, is a bronze $1\frac{1}{2}''$ pattée cross superimposed on a squared surface of rays. On the cross is mounted a four-bladed aircraft propeller. The ribbon of silk *moiré* is predominantly blue with a narrow band of red bordered by white lines in the center. The edges of the ribbon are outlined with equal bands of white inside blue. Succeeding awards are denoted by bronze oak-leaf clusters for Air Force and Army awards and by gold stars for Navy, Marine Corps, and Coast Guard. A miniature enameled metal lapel device may be worn when in civilian attire.

Air Force Manual 900-3, Army Regulation 672-5-1, and Navy Personnel Instructions P1650.1C are the directives covering this award; authorized by Act of Congress, 2 July 1926, and awarded pursuant to Section 8749, Title 10 USC.

AIRMAN'S MEDAL

Plate 17
(p. 38)
The Airman's Medal ranks in precedence with the Soldier's Medal, the Navy and Marine Corps Medal, and the Coast Guard Medal, and was established to provide the Air Force with a distinctive decoration for award in lieu of the Soldier's Medal of the Army. It may be awarded to any member of the United States Armed Forces and to any member of the armed forces of friendly foreign nations who, while serving in any capacity with the Air Force, distinguishes himself by heroism involving voluntary risk of life under conditions other than those of conflict with an armed enemy of the United States. The saving of a life or the success of the voluntary heroic act is not essential for the award.

Contrary to the established practice of creating specially shaped designs for decoration, i.e., stars, crosses, octagon shaped, etc., the AM is in the disk shape ordinarily used for service medals. The pendant is heavier, highly polished, and in excellent relief.

Designed by the Institute of Heraldry, U.S. Army, the Airman's Medal is a 1⅜″ medal officially described as: "Hermes, son of Zeus and representative of youthful vigor and boldness, is depicted releasing an American Bald Eagle, symbolic of the aspirations and ideals of the American airman." An earlier official version referred to the figure as "Mercury" and to the bird as a falcon. Although in mythology, Hermes and Mercury are the same entity, Americans are generally more familiar with the name "Mercury" and the falcon being more representative to Air Force heraldry tends to make the latter version appear to be more apropos. On the reverse is a simple laurel wreath encircling the inscription "FOR VALOR." The ribbon is Brittany Blue displaying alternately in the center 13 vertical stripes of the Air Force colors, golden yellow and ultramarine blue. Succeeding awards are denoted by bronze oak-leaf clusters. A miniature enameled metal lapel device may be worn when in civilian attire.

Air Force Manual 900-3 is the directive covering this award, which stems from the Soldier's Medal Act of 2 July 1926, and is awarded pursuant to Section 8749, Title 10 USC, and Public Law 86–593 of 6 July 1960 which amended Section 8750, Title 10 USC.

COAST GUARD MEDAL

Plate 18
(p. 38)
The Coast Guard Medal may be awarded to any person who, while serving in any capacity with the Coast Guard, distinguishes himself by heroism not involving actual conflict with the enemy. This medal, similar in nature to Army, Navy and Marine Corps medals, is intended primarily for award to military personnel and does not have the same limitations on locale or heroism as the two earlier Coast Guard medals, the silver and gold lifesaving medals (still in existence). The act of courage to earn this medal must have been voluntary and of a nature so as to stand out distinctively. The authority to award the CGM has been delegated to the Secretary of Transportation by the President.

The CGM is of the usual octangular shape within which is a circle of rope. Within the circle in relief is the Coast Guard seal of crossed anchors on which is superimposed a circle. Within the circle is the inscription "UNITED STATES COAST GUARD 1790" and within a smaller inner circle is the United States shield. Small letters above and below the shield spell out "SEMPER PARATUS" (Always Ready).

NAVY AND MARINE CORPS MEDAL

Plate 19
(p. 39)

The Navy and Marine Corps Medal may be awarded to any member of the United States Armed Forces who, while serving in any capacity with the U.S. Navy or Marine Corps including the Reserves, since 6 December 1941, distinguishes himself by heroism not involving actual conflict with an enemy of the United States. In addition, any person to whom the Secretary of the Navy has heretofore awarded a letter of commendation for heroism regardless of the date of such act of heroism, may also be awarded the medal. The saving of a life or the success of the voluntary heroic act is not essential to the award.

Designed by Lt. Cmdr. McClelland, U.S. Navy, and M. A. Crawford (pendant and ribbon, respectively) it is a $1\frac{3}{8}''$ octangular-shaped medal with an eagle with wings unfolded facing to the right. The eagle is astride the shank of an anchor with its right wing partially obscuring the left-facing anchor fluke, under and over which is entwined a rope. Directly below the anchor is a globe depicting the western hemisphere and below that is the inscription "HEROISM." The ribbon incorporates the colors of the Navy and Marine Corps and is from left to right, blue, gold, and scarlet. Succeeding awards are denoted by gold stars.

Navy Personnel Instructions P1650.1C is the directive covering this award; authorized by Act of Congress, 7 August 1942.

SOLDIER'S MEDAL

Plate 20
(p. 39)

The Soldier's Medal may be awarded to any member of the United States Armed Forces and to any member of friendly

1. Air Force Medal of Honor.

2. Army Medal of Honor.

3. Navy, Marine Corps, and Coast Guard Medal of Honor.

4. Air Force Cross.

5 (*front & reverse*). Distinguished Service Cross (Army).

6. Navy Cross.

7. Air Force Distinguished Service Medal.

8. Army Distinguished Service Medal.

9. Coast Guard Distinguished Service Medal.

10. Navy Distinguished Service Medal.

11. Silver Star Medal.

12. Legion of Merit: Chief Commander.

13–15. Legion of Merit: Commander (*center*), Officer (*left*), Legionnaire (*right*).

16. Distinguished Flying Cross.

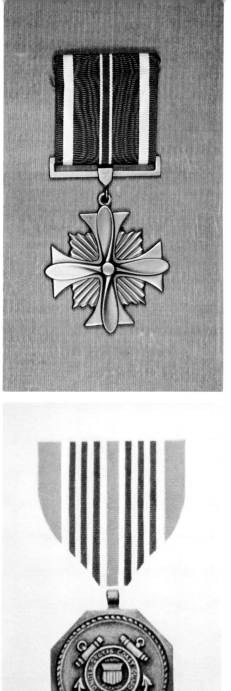

17. Airman's Medal.

18. Coast Guard Medal.

19. Navy and Marine Corps Medal.

20. Soldier's Medal.

21. Bronze Star Medal.

22 (*front & reverse*). Meritorious Service Medal.

23. Air Medal.

24. Joint Service Commendation Medal.

40

25 (*front* & *reverse*). Air Force Commendation Medal.

26. Army Commendation Medal.

27. Coast Guard Commendation Medal.

28. Navy Commendation Medal.

29. Reserve   Special   Commendation Ribbon.

30. Navy Achievement Medal.

31. National Security Medal.

32. Gold Lifesaving Medal.

33. Silver Lifesaving Medal.

34. Secretary of Transportation Commendation for Achievement Ribbon.

35. Badge of Military Merit.

36. Purple Heart.

foreign armed forces who, while serving in any capacity with the U.S. forces, distinguishes himself by heroism involving voluntary risk of life under conditions other than those of conflict with an armed enemy of the United States. The saving of a life or the success of the voluntary heroic act is not essential for the award, nor will awards be made solely on the basis of having saved a life. The award is made in the name of the Secretary of the Army.

Designed by Gaetano Cecere, sculptor of the Army Distinguished Service Medal, the SM is a 1⅜″ octangular-shaped bronze medal bearing an eagle with wings displayed standing on a fasces between two groups of stars of six and seven; above the group of six, a spray of leaves. On the reverse is a shield paly of 13 pieces on the chief, the letters "u.s." supported by sprays of laurel and oak, and around the upper edge the inscription "SOLDIER'S MEDAL," and across the face the inscription "FOR VALOR." The medal is suspended by a rectangular-shaped metal loop with corners rounded from a silk-*moiré* ribbon of two outside stripes of blue and a center of seven white and six red stripes of equal width. Succeeding awards are denoted by bronze oak-leaf clusters. A miniature enameled metal lapel device may be worn when in civilian attire.

Army Regulation 672-5-1 is the directive covering this award; authorized by Act of Congress, 2 July 1926.

BRONZE STAR MEDAL

Plate 21
(p. 39) The Bronze Star Medal may be awarded to any person who, while serving in any capacity with the United States Armed Forces, distinguishes himself either by heroism in surface combat against an armed enemy of the United States or by meritorious achievement not involving participation in aerial flight but in connection with military operations against an enemy. On 24 August 1962, Executive Order 11046 was issued which changed eligibility criteria to provide that the medal could be awarded under one or more of the following conditions: while engaged in an action against an enemy of the United States; while engaged in military operations involving conflict with an opposing foreign force; while serving with friendly foreign forces engaged in armed conflict against an opposing armed force in which the U.S. is not a belligerent party. This latter qualifying criteria now permits cognizance

of heroic deeds or meritorious achievement performed by American servicemen on advisory duty with foreign countries.

The BSM may be awarded upon application to those members of the U.S. Armed Forces who have been previously awarded the Combat Infantrymen or Medical Badge for exemplary conduct in ground combat against an armed enemy of the United States between 7 December 1941 and 2 September 1945, inclusive. The individual's authority to wear one of the badges must be indicated in the application and sent to the Department of the Army for approval.

Designed by Baily, Banks and Biddle, the BSM is a bronze star $1\frac{1}{2}''$ in circumscribing diameter. In the center thereof is a $\frac{3}{16}''$ raised bronze star; the center lines of all rays of both stars coincide. On the reverse is the inscription "HEROIC OR MERITORIOUS ACHIEVEMENT." The star is suspended by a rectangular-shaped loop with corners rounded from a silk-*moiré* ribbon $1\frac{3}{8}''$ wide predominantly red, with a white-edged narrow blue band in the center and white lines at each edge. Succeeding awards are denoted by bronze oak-leaf clusters for Air Force and Army awards and by gold stars for Navy, Marine Corps, and Coast Guard. When awarded for heroism a bronze V is clasped to the suspension ribbon or ribbon bar. A miniature enameled metal replica of the medal ribbon may be worn when in civilian attire.

Air Force Manual 900-3, Army Regulation 672-5-1, and Navy Personnel Instructions P1650.1C are the directives covering this award; authorized by Executive Order 9414, 4 February 1944, which was superseded by Executive Order 11046, 24 August 1962.

MERITORIOUS SERVICE MEDAL

Plate 22
(p. 40)

The Meritorious Service Medal was created just before the end of the Johnson administration for award to United States Armed Forces personnel to recognize outstanding noncombat meritorious achievement or service to the United States. Although the required achievement or service to warrant award of this medal is less than that required for award of the Legion of Merit (p. 27), it must nevertheless be accomplished with distinction above and beyond that required for award of a commendation medal. Some portion of the completed period of service or achievement must have been on or after 16 January 1969.

In combat zones the Bronze Star Medal may be awarded for meritorious service or achievement and ranks between the Legion of Merit and commendation medals; however, there has been no comparable medal available for noncombat situations. This has led, in some cases, to a degradation of the Legion of Merit by awarding it for lesser cause than the original intent, or an award of a commendation medal for services beyond that for which a commendation medal is usually awarded. The medal was suggested by the Navy Decorations and Medals Board.

The MSM is a bronze medal $1\frac{1}{2}''$ in diameter consisting of six rays issuant from the upper three points of a five-pointed star with beveled edges containing two smaller stars defined by incised outlines; in front of the lower part of the star is an eagle with wings upraised standing upon two upward curving branches of laurel tied with a ribbon between the feet of the eagle. The ribbon is mainly ruby with white vertical stripes with ruby lines at each edge. Succeeding awards are denoted by bronze oak-leaf clusters for Air Force and Army awards and by gold stars for Navy, Marine Corps, and Coast Guard.

Air Force Manual 900-3, Army Regulation 672-5-1, Coast Guard Personnel Manual CG-207, and Navy Personnel Instructions P1650.1C are the directives covering this award; authorized by Executive Order on 17 January 1969.

AIR MEDAL

Plate 23 (p. 40) The Air Medal may be awarded to any person who, after 8 September 1939, while serving in any capacity with the United States Armed Forces, distinguishes himself by meritorious achievement while participating in aerial flight. The medal may also be awarded for single acts or sustained operational activities against an enemy of the United States. It may be awarded to members of foreign armed services and also to both U.S. and foreign civilians.

Some members of the armed services have earned and been awarded this medal 50 times, and perhaps far more than that. Since it is ordinarily possible to show award of only 31 medals on a single ribbon, I inquired at the Awards Section of the Air Force to find out what one does when he has more than 31 Air Medals. An official of that department informed me that one simply wears an additional Air Medal ribbon, placing the appropriate number of oak-leaf clusters thereon. Later this information was promulgated by an amendment to Air Force Manual 900-3.

It may seem unusual to the reader that an individual may be awarded one decoration so many times. The Air Medal is awarded most often for sustained airborne activities. Determination of how many and what type missions must be flown to earn the medal vary with each branch of the services. The intensity of enemy air activity and opposition encountered play a large role in these determinations. During World War II, criteria differed in the various theaters of operation because of the variance in dangers involved by enemy resistance. In one command, a man flew 10 missions to earn the original medal and earned an oak-leaf cluster or gold star for each subsequent five missions. Thus men who flew a standard 100-mission tour could earn 19 Air Medals in the process of completing their missions, plus additional Air Medals for individual acts, such as downing an enemy aircraft or some other outstanding feat. Many of these men went on to the Korean and Vietnam wars, where they earned more and more awards.

In the Vietnam War the Air Medal has been awarded to a far wider range of personnel than ever before. Many "noncombat" members earned the medal by participating in helicopter missions and rescues. A unique Air Force group amassed a large number of Air Medals, plus other decorations by voluntarily serving as "flare kickers" aboard night-flying aircraft. These men loaded and dropped flares on enemy areas from aircraft in support of beleaguered friendly forces. What made them unusual was that they worked standard 12-hour days, seven-day weeks in ground jobs, such as clerks, cooks, personnel technicians, etc., and flew the flare-dropping missions voluntarily without recompense in either money or time. After 1967, however, Air Force authorities barred ground personnel from participating in aerial missions.

A group of dedicated people earned the Air Medal for flying Sub-Patrol missions along the U.S. coastline during World War II. The unusual aspect of their decoration was that all were civilians when they earned it and some were men of advanced age. They were Civil Air Patrol pilots who gave their time, their personal aircraft, and, for several months, even paid for their fuel out of their own pockets. They did an excellent job, sinking at least one enemy submarine and sighting countless others. Some time after World War II, a grateful U.S. Air Force recognized the services of these patriotic and selfless men by awarding them the Air Medal.

Designed by Walter K. Hancock, this striking and beautiful medal is a bronze compass rose $1\frac{11}{16}''$ in circumscribing diameter suspended by the pointer and charged with an eagle volant carrying a lightning bolt in each talon. The points of the compass rose on the reverse are modeled, with the central portion plain. The medal is suspended from a silk-*moiré* ribbon of bands of ultramarine blue and golden orange.

Succeeding awards of the medal to Air Force and Army personnel are denoted by bronze oak-leaf clusters. Since 28 February 1964, a V device can be worn on the Air Medal by Army personnel when the medal is awarded for heroic or valorous deeds. As of this writing the Air Force and Navy have not yet authorized the wearing of the V device on the medal. However, Navy and Marine Corps personnel have been authorized still another pair of devices to be worn on the Air Medal ribbon. On 14 November 1967, the Secretary of the Navy authorized "Distinguishing devices for Strike/Flight awards of the Air Medal." These devices are to distinguish between "single achievement" awards and those for completion of a set number of missions. The additional devices are a bronze $\frac{3}{16}''$ star and Arabic numerals. When earned for a single achievement, the Air Medal ribbon will be worn with a bronze star affixed to it. If a second "single achievement" medal is earned, a $\frac{5}{16}''$ gold star replaces the smaller bronze star. Arabic numerals are worn to show Air Medal awards earned for a set number of missions. For example, if a man had earned two "single achievement" awards and three "sustained activity" awards, he would have one $\frac{5}{16}''$ gold star and the Arabic numeral 3 on his ribbon. This change is retroactive to all awards earned after 9 April 1962.

Air Force Manual 900-3, Army Regulation 672-5-1, and Navy Personnel Instructions P1650.1C are the directives covering this award; authorized by Executive Order 9158, 11 May 1942 as amended by Executive Order 9242-a, 11 September 1942.

JOINT SERVICE COMMENDATION MEDAL

Plate 24
(p. 40)
The Joint Service Commendation Medal may be awarded to any member of the United States Armed Forces who distinguishes himself by meritorious service or achievement. It is awarded in the name of the Secretary of Defense. Ordinarily, one must be serving with the Office of the Secretary of Defense, Joint Chiefs of Staff, Defense Supply Agency, National Security Agency, or in a joint task force, command, or control group. The degree of merit need not be unique, but must be distinctive.

Designed by the Institute of Heraldry, U.S. Army, the JSCM is an exceptionally well-designed wrought medal device consisting of four conjoined hexagons—two vertically and two horizontally—of green enamel. Centered on the medal is an eagle with wings displayed and its chest is charged with the shield of the United States; the eagle is grasping three arrows in its talons (as depicted on the seal of the Department of Defense). At the top are 13 gold stars; at the bottom, a gold-stylized heraldic delineation representing land, sea, and air, all within a gold circular laurel wreath bound with gold bands $1\frac{5}{8}''$ in diameter, with the areas between the inside of the wreath and the device pierced.

Air Force Manual 900-3, Army Regulation 672-5-1, and Navy Personnel Instructions P1650.1C are the directives covering this award; authorized by Department of Defense Directive 1348.14, 25 June 1963 and Section 1121, Title 10 USC.

COMMENDATION MEDAL

AIR FORCE

Plate 25
(p. 41)
The Air Force Commendation Medal may be awarded to any member of the United States Armed Forces who, while serving in any capacity with the Air Force after 24 March 1958, distinguishes himself by meritorious achievement or meritorious service. The degree of merit need not be unique, but it must be distinctive. Acts of courage that do not meet the requirements for award of the Airman's Medal may be considered for award of an AFCM. It may not be awarded to generals or flag officers for achievement or services performed while serving in those grades. It may be awarded to foreign

military personnel, but only with the sanction of the Department of the Air Force. Civilians are not eligible for this award.

Designed by the Institute of Heraldry, U.S. Air Force, the AFCM is a 1⅜" bronze hexagon medallion bearing eagle, shield, and arrows from the seal of the Department of the Air Force. On the reverse below the inscription "FOR MILITARY MERIT" is a panel to inscribe the recipient's name. The ribbon is predominantly yellow with blue edges and three bands of blue spaced in the center.

Air Force Manual 900-3 is the directive covering this award; authorized by the Secretary of the Air Force and Department of the Air Force General Order No. 16, 28 March 1958.

ARMY

Plate 26 (p. 41) The Army Commendation Medal, first known as the Commendation Ribbon and later as the Army Commendation Ribbon with Medal Pendant, was redesignated to its present title by Department of the Army General Order No. 10 on 31 March 1960. It may be awarded to any member of the United States Armed Forces who, while serving in any capacity with the U.S. Army, distinguishes himself by meritorious service or meritorious achievement. The degree of merit or achievement of the individual should be of such magnitude that it clearly places one above his peers. Acts of courage that do not meet the requirements for awards of the Soldier's Medal or the Bronze Star Medal may be considered as evidence of a meritorious achievement warranting award of an ACM.

Army Regulation 672-5-1 states that the Army Commendation Medal will not be awarded to general officers. The award of the medal may be made to any individual commended after 6 December 1941 and prior to 1 January 1946 in a letter, certificate, or order of commendation signed by an officer in the grade or position of a major general or higher.

Second and succeeding awards are shown by bronze oak-leaf clusters. Since 29 February 1964, personnel who were awarded the Army Commendation Medal for heroic or valorous deeds have been authorized to wear the V device on the ribbon. A miniature metal replica of the ribbon may be worn with civilian attire.

Designed by the Institute of Heraldry, U.S. Army, the ACM is a 1⅜" bronze hexagon (one point up) bearing an

American Bald Eagle with wings displayed horizontally grasping in its talons three crossed arrows, and on its breast, a shield paly of 13 pieces and a chief. On the reverse between the inscriptions "FOR MILITARY" and "MERIT" a panel, all above a sprig of laurel. The ribbon is green and white on silk *moiré*.

Army Regulation 672-5-1 is the directive covering this award; authorized by the Secretary of War, 18 December 1945, and amended title from Department of the Army General Order No. 10, 31 March 1960.

COAST GUARD

Plate 27
(p. 42) The Coast Guard Commendation Medal, formerly titled the Coast Guard Commendation Ribbon with Medal Pendant, has since been redesignated to its present title. The Secretary of Transportation or the Commandant, U.S. Coast Guard, may award the CGCM to any member of the United States Armed Forces who, while serving in any capacity with the Coast Guard, distinguishes himself by meritorious service resulting in unusual and outstanding achievement rendered with the Coast Guard serving under Transportation Department jurisdiction.

The CGCM is a 1⅜″ hexagon within which is a circle of rope. Inside the circle is a stylized American Bald Eagle, facing right, and superimposed on the eagle in relief is the Coast Guard seal of crossed anchors with a circle imposed on the anchors. Within the circle are the words "UNITED STATES COAST GUARD 1790" and within a smaller inner circle is the United States shield. Small letters above and below the shield spell out "SEMPER PARATUS" (Always Ready). The ribbon is green and white with three inner stripes of white. Succeeding awards are denoted by gold stars.

Coast Guard Personnel Manual CG-207 is the directive covering this award, the ribbon of which was originally authorized by the Secretary of the Treasury, 26 August 1947; the medal pendant, 5 July 1951.

NAVY

Plate 28
(p. 42) The Navy Commendation Medal, formerly known as the Commendation Ribbon with Medal Pendant, may be awarded to any member of the Navy, Marine Corps, and Coast Guard who has received an individual letter of commendation signed

by the Secretary of the Navy, Commander-in-Chief, U.S. Pacific or Atlantic Fleet, for an act of heroism or service performed between 6 December 1941 and 11 January 1944, and to any person of the Navy, Marine Corps, and Coast Guard who has received a commendation signed by the Secretary of the Navy or other designated authority, provided the letter of commendation specifically authorizes the NCM.

Designed by the Quartermaster Corps, Institute of Heraldry, U.S. Army, the NCM pendant ($1\frac{3}{8}''$) is exactly the same as that of the Army Commendation Medal. The ribbon has the same colors—green and white—but has only two white stripes at each end. Succeeding awards are denoted by gold stars. A bronze letter V is worn on the medal to show that it was earned while participating in operations against an armed enemy.

Navy Personnel Instructions P1650.1C is the directive covering this award; authorized by ALNAV Message No. 11, 11 January 1944.

RESERVE SPECIAL COMMENDATION RIBBON

Plate 29
(p. 42)

The Reserve Special Commendation Ribbon was established for award to those officers of the Organized Reserve who officially commanded in a meritorious manner for a period of four years between 1 January 1930 and 7 December 1941, an organized battalion, squadron, or separate division of the Naval Reserve, or an organized battalion or squadron of the Marine Corps Reserve and had a total service in the Reserve of a least 10 years. Four years of commanding such units were required for award of the ribbon; however, they need not have been continuous.

The ribbon is of standard size with the colors dark blue, yellow, red, olive green, red, yellow, and dark blue in widths of two, two, eight, seven, eight, two, and two millimeters.

Navy and Marine Corps Awards Manual (revised 1953) is the directive covering this award; authorized by the Secretary of the Navy, 16 April 1946.

NAVY ACHIEVEMENT MEDAL

Plate 30
(p. 42)
The Navy Achievement Medal, which in precedence ranks just below the Navy Commendation Medal, was formerly

titled the "Navy Commendation for Achievement" and was previously only a ribbon. It may be awarded to enlisted and commissioned members of the Navy and Marine Corps, including reserves who are serving in the grade of lieutenant commander or major and below. It may also be awarded to persons in the other armed services of comparable grade when attached to or serving with the Navy. It is awarded for professional or leadership achievement in a combat or noncombat situation based on sustained performance or specific achievement of a superlative nature. A V device may be worn on the $1\frac{3}{8}''$ ribbon if the recipient is cited for acts or services involving direct participation in combat operations.

The NAM is of a distinct square shape with beveled corners and the device for attachment to the ribbon is an integral part of the pendant design. In relief on the $1\frac{1}{4}''$ medal are four five-pointed stars, one at each corner and imposed in the center is the stylized naval anchor entwined with rope.

Authority is contained in SECNAVNOTE 1650, 17 July 1967; SECNAVINST 1650.1C, 16 August 1963; and SECNAVINST 1650.28, 17 July 1967.

COAST GUARD ACHIEVEMENT MEDAL

The Coast Guard Achievement Medal is awarded to Coast Guard personnel under essentially the same conditions as are required for the Navy Achievement Medal. It may also be awarded to persons in the other armed services when attached to or serving with the Coast Guard. It is given for professional or leadership achievements in a combat or noncombat situation based on sustained performance or specific achievement of a superlative nature.

A V device may be worn on the ribbon if the recipient is cited for acts or services involving direct participation in combat operations.

Authority for award is contained in Coast Guard Personnel Manual CG 207.

NATIONAL SECURITY MEDAL

Plate 31
(p. 43) The National Security Medal, essentially an award of a civilian agency, is briefly covered here since the first recipients of the

award were military personnel and also because military personnel will probably continue to become eligible for its award in the future.

The NSM is awarded to any person without regard to nationality, including members of the United States Armed Forces, for distinguished achievements or outstanding contributions, on or after 26 July 1947, in the field of intelligence relating to national security. The contribution may be either exceptionally meritorious service performed in a position of high responsibility or an act of valor requiring personal courage of a high degree and complete disregard of personal safety.

Designed by the United States Mint, this rarely awarded and unusual medal is a blue-enameled compass rose surrounded by a red-enameled oval, the interior dimensions of which are 1″ vertically and ⅞″ horizontally, bearing the inscriptions "UNITED STATES OF AMERICA" at the top and "NATIONAL SECURITY" at the bottom. The whole is enclosed within a laurel wreath of gold-finished bronze surmounted by an American Bald Eagle standing with wings raised. On the reverse a serial number appears on the eagle and the inscription "PRESENTED TO" are impressed on the compass rose. The name of the recipient is engraved below. The medal is suspended by a loop from a silk-*moiré* ribbon of dark blue and gold, with diagonal gold lines extending downward from the wearer's right to left across the center of the band of dark blue.

Authority was Executive Order 10431, 19 January 1953.

LIFESAVING MEDAL

The lifesaving medals are available to members of the United States Armed Forces, but they are rarely awarded to military personnel because of the existence of medals in all services whose criteria for award are very similar.

Gold—First Class

Plate 32 (p. 43) The Gold Lifesaving Medal is awarded by the Transportation Department to civilians and members of the U.S. Armed Forces alike who endanger their lives in saving or attempting to save lives of others from dangers of the sea.

Silver—Second Class

Plate 33
(p. 43) The Silver Lifesaving Medal is awarded under the same general conditions as the Gold; however, it is secondary in importance and permits a lesser degree of heroism for award.

*   *   *

The illustrations of the medals display only the new ribbons and pendants of these particular medals. The suspension ribbons shown are not those which were established originally with the medal. Since their creation, there have been several changes. The width of the ribbons and the pendants have been reduced in size, and the ribbon has been changed in design and color to the examples you see on the two pendants in the illustrations. Currently, the only authorized ribbons for wear are those most recently devised. The ribbons now are $1\frac{3}{8}''$ wide and the pendants are about $1\frac{1}{2}''$ in diameter.

Designed by Anthony C. Paquet, a designer of the Medal of Honor, these medals, when reduced in design and size, retained the salient features of the originals. The obverse of both medals is beautifully executed, although difficult to photograph in such a manner as to reveal their fine detail. The obverse of the gold medal has in the background a wrecked ship. In bas-relief in the foreground are three men in a boat beset by high waves; one man standing is extending a spar to still another person who is adrift; one man is rowing and another casting a rope to a survivor. Within the inner and outer rims of the obverse are the words "UNITED STATES OF AMERICA" and "ACT OF CONGRESS AUGUST 4, 1949." The obverse of the silver medal shows a traditionally styled woman suspended in the air, extending a sash to a man afloat in high seas. The inscription around the rim of the medal is identical to that of the gold medal.

Authority was 14 USC 500 and Act of Congress, 4 August 1949.

SECRETARY OF TRANSPORTATION COMMENDATION FOR ACHIEVEMENT RIBBON

Plate 34
(p. 44) The Secretary of Transportation Commendation for Achievement Ribbon, formerly titled the Secretary of the Treasury

Commendation for Achievement Award, is authorized for wear by military personnel. The award is intended to recognize professional achievement which exceeds that normally expected considering the individual's grade, training, experience, and job requirements. It is to recognize management and technical achievement that is beneficial to the Department of Transportation.

Designed by the Institute of Heraldry, U.S. Army, the $1\frac{3}{8}''$ ribbon is green with orange and white stripes. There is no pendant.

Authority was Department of Transportation Order DOT 3400.1, 27 July 1967.

PURPLE HEART

Plates 35, 36 (p. 44) The Purple Heart, a highly respected decoration of the United States Armed Forces, occupies a very unique position. The decoration can be earned in only one way—by being wounded. An attendant requirement is that the wound must have been received as a direct result of enemy action.

Stemming directly from Gen. George Washington's Badge of Military Merit, the Purple Heart is our oldest military decoration. As mentioned earlier in this chapter, the Badge of Military Merit was awarded for gallantry or extraordinary fidelity and essential service. Upon its revival in 1932, as the Purple Heart, the decoration was to be awarded in two categories: the first, "For acts or services performed prior to 22 February 1932, the Purple Heart is confined to those persons, who, as members of the Army, were awarded the Meritorious Services Citation Certificate by the Commander-in-Chief, American Expeditionary Forces, or who were wounded in action in any war or campaign under conditions which entitle them to wear a wound chevron." The second category provided for those persons who, after 22 February 1932, while serving in the United States Army, perform any singularly meritorious act of extraordinary fidelity or essential service.

Thus there may be a number of older persons who have the Purple Heart without having been wounded. But the number is probably very small, since early in World War II recipients of the Purple Heart who had been awarded the medal for meritorious service were given the opportunity to exchange the Purple Heart for a more appropriate decoration.

In 1942, President Franklin D. Roosevelt issued Executive Order 9277 which provided that the Purple Heart would be made available to members of all the armed services who were wounded in action. After that the Purple Heart was awarded exclusively for wounds received as a direct result of enemy action. Currently, the Purple Heart may be awarded to members of the United States Armed Forces and to civilian citizens of the U.S., who, while serving with the armed forces, are wounded. Multiple wounds received at the same time are counted as a basis for only one award.

Designed by Elizabeth Will and sculpted by John R. Sinnock, then Chief Engraver of the Philadelphia Mint, the PH is a purple heart within a bronze border bearing a profile head in relief of Gen. George Washington in military uniform. Above the heart is the shield of General Washington's coat of arms between two sprays of leaves in green enamel. On the reverse below the shield and leaves without enamel is a raised bronze heart with the inscription "FOR MILITARY MERIT." The entire device is $1\frac{11}{16}''$ long. The medal is suspended by a rectangular-shaped loop with corners rounded from a silk-*moiré* ribbon of pansy purple and white. Succeeding awards are denoted by bronze oak-leaf clusters for Air Force and Army personnel and by gold stars for Navy, Marine Corps, and Coast Guard.

Air Force Manual 900-3, Army Regulation 672-5-1, and Navy Personnel Instructions P1650.1C are the directives covering this award; authorized by War Department General Order No. 3, 1932 and Executive Order 11016, 25 April 1962.

MERCHANT MARINE DECORATIONS

DISTINGUISHED SERVICE MEDAL

Plate 37
(p. 61)
The Merchant Marine Distinguished Service Medal was the highest Merchant Marine award authorized. Personnel, who after 3 September 1939 distinguished themselves by outstanding service in the line of duty, could be awarded this medal, which is suspended on a $1\frac{3}{8}''$ ribbon. During World War II, 175 of these medals were awarded.

Designed by Paul Manship, the MMDSM was authorized by Act of Congress, 11 April 1942.

MERITORIOUS SERVICE MEDAL

Plate 38
(p. 61)
The Meritorious Service Medal was awarded to Merchant Marine personnel who were commended by the Administrator of the War Shipping Administration for meritorious service; 424 such medals were awarded.

Paul Manship also designed this medal, authorized by Presidential Executive Order on 29 August 1944.

MARINER'S MEDAL

Plate 39
(p. 61)
The Mariner's Medal was awarded to personnel serving on a Merchant ship who were wounded, injured, or suffered through hazardous exposure as a result of actions by enemy forces.

The Mariner's Medal was also designed by Paul Manship, and was authorized by Act of Congress, 10 May 1943.

48 (*front & reverse*). Navy Expeditionary Medal.

49 (*front & reverse*). Marine Corps Expeditionary Medal.

65

50. NC-4 Medal.

51 (*front & reverse*). Yangtze Service Medal.

52 (*front & reverse*). Second Nicaraguan Campaign Medal.

66

53. Byrd Antarctic Expedition Medal.

54. Second Byrd Antarctic Expedition Medal.

55. (*front & reverse*). China Service Medal.

56 (*front & reverse*). United States Antarctic Expedition Medal.

57. American Defense Service Medal.

58 (*front & reverse*). American Campaign Medal.

68

59 (*front & reverse*). Asiatic-Pacific Campaign Medal.

60 (*front & reverse*). European-African-Middle Eastern Campaign Medal.

61. Women's Army Corps Service Medal.

62 (*front & reverse*). World War II Victory Medal.

63 (*front & reverse*). Army of Occupation Medal (*right*).

64 (*front & reverse*). Navy Occupation Service Medal.

65 (*front & reverse*). Medal for Humane Action.

66 (*front & reverse*). National Defense Service Medal.

67 (*front & reverse*). Korean Service Medal.

68 (*front & reverse*). Antarctica Service Medal.

2

U. S. SERVICE AND CAMPAIGN MEDALS

United States Service and Campaign medals have not had as long a history as our other decorations but their part in the military pageantry is no less important. The Civil War was the first campaign for which a United States campaign medal was authorized, but it was not until 1905 that Congress created the medal. Since the Civil War Campaign Medal (p. 136) was originally devised, more than 74 different campaign and service awards, medals, and ribbons have been designed for award and issue.

Campaign and service medals are treated together here because of their similarity in design and reason for award. Primarily, a service medal is awarded for the service of an individual; that is, the Army Good Conduct Medal (p. 76) is awarded for a certain period of "Honor, Efficiency and Fidelity" performed by the recipient; the World War II Victory Medal (p. 92) for a specified period of service performed honorably on or before 31 December 1946.

A campaign medal is an award for having participated in a specific battle engagement or campaign. An example would be the Second Nicaraguan Campaign Medal (p. 83) which was for service from 27 August 1926 to 2 January 1933.

Since there were so many battles, engagements, and campaigns during both world wars, the job of determining and designing individual medals for each skirmish would have required a separate army of designers, sculptors, and metalsmiths for one theater of operations alone. As a result, World War I produced only one campaign medal; World War II produced only three—the American, the Asiatic-Pacific, and the European-African-Middle Eastern campaign medals—with individual battles and campaigns marked by means of

73

devices (stars and arrowheads) worn on the theater campaign medal.

Following World War II, there have been only two combat actions that have merited individual medallic recognition—the Korean and Vietnam wars—resulting in issuance of the Korean and Vietnam service medals. Other skirmishes and combat actions that the U.S. has engaged in, in recent years, are marked by the fairly new Armed Forces Expeditionary Medal (p. 98).

The following pages briefly describe all U.S. service and campaign medals that can be worn on the uniform of a member of the active service today. Though it will appear in a few cases that the awards shown could be worn only by a septuagenarian, it is possible that many older career members possess these awards and they should therefore be included.

COMBAT READINESS MEDAL

Plate 40
(p. 62)

The Combat Readiness Medal is awarded to members of the Air Force who are combat-ready aircraft-crew members for a four-year period. The term "combat ready" is defined as being professionally or technically qualified in an aircraft-crew position in an aircraft which can be used in combat. Members of missile-launch crews are also eligible. Serving in combat is not required.

When first established, the CRM was classified as a decoration, ranking over the service commendation medals, the lifesaving medals, and the Purple Heart. This was a unique decoration in the history of U.S. awards in that persons who qualified for the award were not required to distinguish themselves by the usual standards of achievement, meritorious service, or heroism. They merely met training and professional standards in their particular skill and maintained them for a four-year period. Even the lowest ranking decoration of all, the Purple Heart, required physical presence in a combat area and, in almost every case, engagement with an armed enemy.

Several months after the CRM was created and its precedence established, the author took exception to the precedence and in fact to the entire idea of ranking such an award as a "decoration" rather than a service medal. A recommendation was submitted to the Awards Branch of Air Force Headquarters, setting out long-established Air Force policy and pointing out the fallacy of ranking a service-type award over other earned decorations, and recommending that the medal's place be restructured to conform with accepted practice and tradition. Finally, in September 1967, after the author's original recommendations had been buttressed by similar recommendations from highly placed officials throughout the Air Force, the Awards Branch of the Air Force realigned the medal to its present position as the top-ranking service medal.

Designed by the Institute of Heraldry, U.S. Army, this $1\frac{1}{2}''$ medal, simple in design yet handsome, has its description as encircling a ring of stylized cloud forms, a border of concentric rays, its rim concave between 12 points, charged with six arrowheads, alternating with the points of two triangular flight symbols having centerlines ridged conversely. One is pointed south and overlapping, and the other pointed north with the apex extending beyond the rim, becoming the point of suspension of the medal. The ribbon is predominantly Old Glory Red and is banded in blue, with a narrow dark blue stripe separated by two wider stripes of light blue. Succeeding awards are denoted by bronze oak-leaf clusters.

Air Force Manual 900-3 is the directive covering this award; authorized by a directive of the Secretary of the Air Force on 9 March 1964 with effective date of 1 August 1964, as amended on 28 August 1967.

GOOD CONDUCT MEDAL

AIR FORCE

Plate 41
(p. 62)
Well over 15 years after the Air Force became an autonomous service, it finally created its own Good Conduct Medal. The medal is awarded for three-year periods of "Honor, Efficiency and Fidelity." During periods of war or national emergency, it may be awarded for periods of one year or less.

Those Air Force members who previously were awarded the Army Good Conduct Medal will continue to wear the Army medal with any bronze or silver loops earned prior to 1 June 1963. After 1 June 1963, all awards made for periods of service terminating after that date will be for the Air Force Good Conduct Medal. Those persons who for some reason were not awarded Good Conduct medals for service which terminated prior to 1 June 1963, will continue to be awarded the Army version.

The Air Force did not exercise much ingenuity in this particular medal. The pendant is identical to the Army Good Conduct Medal, and only the ribbon differs. Cost consciousness probably dictated this action since the medal's cost (to the government) is some $.10 less than the Army GCM.

Designed by Joseph Kiselewski, the metal is bronze, $1\frac{1}{4}''$ in diameter. On the obverse is an eagle standing on a closed book and Roman sword, encircled by the inscription "EFFICIENCY-HONOR-FIDELITY." On the reverse is a five-pointed star and scroll between the inscription "FOR GOOD" and "CONDUCT," surrounded by a wreath formed by a laurel branch on the left and an oak branch on the right. The medal is suspended by a ring from a silk-*moiré* ribbon, designed by the Institute of Heraldry, U.S. Army, of predominantly light blue with narrow vertical stripes of red, white, and blue to the right and left of the center. Succeeding awards are denoted by bronze and silver oak-leaf clusters.

Air Force Manual 900-3 is the directive covering this award; authorized by the Secretary of the Air Force, effective 1 June 1963, based on Executive Order 10444, 10 April 1953.

ARMY

Plate 42 (p. 62) The Army Good Conduct Medal is awarded to enlisted members of the United States Army for three-year periods of "Honor, Efficiency and Fidelity." During limited periods of World War II and the Korean War, the initial award of the GCM could be made for periods of less than three years. It also may be awarded at this time to those persons separating from the service sooner than three years if their separation was by reason of physical disability incurred in the line of duty.

The medal had its origin in the "Badge of Military Distinction," another award created by Gen. George Washington during the Revolution. This original award was in the form of a narrow strip of white cloth to be awarded to noncommissioned officers and other enlisted ranks for service of three or more years of "bravery, fidelity and good conduct." Although these badges were similar to service stripes (hashmarks) worn today, the intent of the distinction parallels the criteria of the GCM. The pendant to the medal is exactly the same as the Air Force Good Conduct Medal. The ribbon, designed by

Arthur E. Dubois, is dark red silk, with three white stripes bordering each edge. Succeeding awards are denoted by bronze, silver, and gold clasps. A second award would be indicated by a bronze clasp with two loops or knots, a sixth by a silver clasp with one loop, and an 11th by a gold clasp with one loop.

It is unlikely that many gold clasps will ever be seen since the first one could not be awarded until 26 August 1970, 33 years after the medal was created. The initial regulations provided that persons accruing three years' qualifying service on or after 26 August 1940 could be awarded the medal. Since most men leave the service after they have completed the 20-year retirement qualifications, these gold clasps will be rare.

Army Regulation 672-5-1, and, when appropriate, Air Force Manual 900-3, are the directives covering this award; authorized by Executive Order 8809, 28 June 1941, as amended by Executive Order 9323, 31 March 1943, and Executive Order 10444, 10 April 1953.

COAST GUARD

Plate 43
(p. 63) The Coast Guard Good Conduct Medal is awarded to enlisted personnel for three-year periods of good conduct and demonstrated proficiency. Originally authorized on 12 December 1923, award of the medal was made retroactive to personnel having qualifying service as early as 17 May 1920. First awarded for four-year service, criteria was changed, effective 1 July 1934, to the present three-year qualifying period.

Following the traditional design of Navy and Coast Guard awards, the $1\frac{1}{2}''$ pendant is round, has a chain as an inner circle, another circle made of rope, and between the chain and rope encircled on the medal is the inscription "SEMPER PARATUS" (Always Ready). Within the rope circle is the Coast Guard seal of crossed anchors, with a circle imposed on the anchors. Within the circle is the inscription "UNITED STATES COAST GUARD 1790," and within a smaller inner circle is the United States shield. At the bottom of the medal below the inner rope circle are crossed oars. The ribbon is a deep maroon with a single white stripe. Succeeding awards are denoted by bronze stars.

Coast Guard Personnel Manual CG-207 is the directive covering this award; authorized by SECNAVINST 1650.1C.

MARINE CORPS

Plate 44
(p. 63)

The Marine Corps Good Conduct Medal is currently awarded to enlisted personnel who are distinguished for obedience, sobriety, industry, courage, neatness, and proficiency for three-year periods. Like the Navy Good Conduct Medal, criteria for this award has changed many times over the years since 20 July 1896, when the Marine Corps inaugurated Special Order No. 49 which said in part "That any man holding an excellent discharge shall, upon reenlistment, when recommended by the commanding officer of a ship or the commanding officer of Marines at a shore station, and a board of three officers ordered by the Colonel Commandant, United States Marine Corps, receive a Good Conduct Medal. . . . Good Conduct Medals are given in recognition of good behavior and faithful service, and no person shall be deprived of them, or of the advantages attached to them, except by sentence of a general court martial."

Designed by Maj. Gen. Charles Heywood, USMC, the $1\frac{1}{4}''$ medal has a distinctive attachment in that the medal pendant is suspended from a miniature rifle which is attached to the suspension ribbon. The pendant has an inner ring of chain identical to that of the Navy Good Conduct Medal and has the traditional naval anchor emplaced within the chain. The anchor is tilted at a slight angle to the left. The entire shank has imposed on it an inner circle of rope, and within that circle is a representation of a Marine gunner immediately to the rear of an old style naval gun. A scroll, resting between the flukes of the anchor bears the words "SEMPER FIDELIS" (Always Faithful). The reverse has a plain inner circle in which the inscription "FIDELITY, ZEAL, OBEDIENCE" appears. At the very top is a shield-shaped form in relief without any internal design. Within the inner circle, the space is left blank for engraving.

Until recent years, an inscribed bar clasp was awarded for second and subsequent awards, but presently bronze stars are worn on both the suspension ribbon and the ribbon bar. At one time, the second and subsequent awards were denoted on the ribbon bar by use of bronze Arabic numerals.

Authority is USMC General Order 49, 20 July 1896, and SECNAVINST 1650.1C.

NAVY

Plate 45
(p. 63) The Navy Good Conduct Medal is awarded to recognize four-year periods of good conduct and above average duty proficiency of enlisted men. Prior to 1 November 1963, the Navy required only three-year qualifying periods. In the 100 years since its creation as a badge on 26 April 1869, the criteria has changed appreciably and the *Navy and Marine Corps Awards Manual* devotes several pages of fine type to this award.

Designed by the U.S. Mint, this was the first good conduct medal authorized in any of the services and has retained its present design since 13 July 1892, when it was redesigned. The $1\frac{1}{4}''$ pendant is a deep bronze color, with a chain in relief in a circle around the circumference of the medal. Inside the chain is the traditional naval anchor on which is imposed a circle of rope with a sailing ship within the circle. Below the ship is the name "CONSTITUTION." Between the chain and the rope are the words "UNITED STATES" and on the anchor the word "NAVY." The reverse has the words "FIDELITY, ZEAL, OBEDIENCE."

Until recent years, the medal was suspended from the ribbon by a bar similar to that employed by the Distinguished Flying Cross (p. 30), but it is now the usual shape of the other service medals. Clasps were formerly authorized but no longer are. Those persons having the clasps may retain them but they cannot be worn on the ribbon. Succeeding awards are denoted by bronze and silver stars.

Authority was established by the Secretary of the Navy on 26 April 1869 and the present regulation is SECNAVINST 1650.1C.

WORLD WAR I VICTORY MEDAL

Plate 46
(p. 64) The World War I Victory Medal was awarded for service in the Army, Navy, or Marine Corps between 6 April 1917 and 11 November 1918, or for later service between 12 November 1918 and 5 August 1919 with the American Expeditionary Forces in European Russia. In was also awarded for service in the American Expeditionary Forces in Siberia between 12

SERVICE AND CAMPAIGN MEDALS **79**

November 1918 and 1 April 1920. There were three types of clasps awarded for wear with the medal. (These are discussed in Chapter 8.) In all the services bronze stars worn on the ribbon bar indicated the issuance of a clasp; silver stars represented a citation for gallantry.

The 14 Allied nations decided on a single ribbon, but pendant design was left up to each nation. James E. Fraser was the designer of the U.S. pendant, which is a bronze medal 36 mm. in diameter. On the obverse is a Winged Victory. On the reverse are the words "THE GREAT WAR FOR CIVILIZATION," the coat of arms of the United States, and the names of Allied and associated nations. The ribbon is of silk *moiré* and is 36 mm. wide, composed of two rainbows placed in juxtaposition and having the red in the middle with a white thread along each edge.

Authority is Act of Congress, 1919, and promulgated to the armed services by Navy Department General Order Number 482 of 30 July 1919 and War Department General Order 48, 1919.

ARMY OF OCCUPATION OF GERMANY MEDAL (WORLD WAR I)

Plate 47 The Army of Occupation of Germany Medal was awarded
(p. 64) by the United States Army for service with the occupation forces in Germany and Austria between 12 November 1918 and 11 July 1923. Personnel of the Navy and Marine Corps were also eligible for the award of the medal by the Army, if they were attached or assigned to Army units in Germany or Austria between the cited dates.

Designed by Trygve A. Rovelstad, the medal is of bronze, $1\frac{1}{4}''$ in diameter. On the obverse is a profile of General of the Armies John J. Pershing. Around the upper edge are four five-pointed stars, on the left the words, "GENERAL JOHN J. PERSHING," and on the right an unsheathed sword, point up, within a laurel wreath with the years "1918" and "1923." On the reverse is an eagle standing on Castle Ehrenbreitstein within a circle composed of the words "U.S. ARMY OF OCCUPATION OF GERMANY" and three five-pointed stars. The medal is suspended from a ring attached to a silk-*moiré* ribbon of blue, red, white, and black. When first designed, the ribbon ends, instead of being vertical in design, were wavy. This was changed shortly after authorization of the medal for some unknown reason. No appurtenances or devices are authorized for wear on the ribbon bar or suspension ribbon.

Authority is Act of Congress, 21 November 1941 (55 Stat. 781), and promulgated by War Department Bulletin 34, 1941.

EXPEDITIONARY MEDALS OF THE NAVY AND MARINE CORPS

The Expeditionary Medals of the Navy and Marine Corps are awarded to members who have actually landed on foreign territory and engaged in operations against armed opposition, or operated under circumstances which, after full consideration, were deemed to merit special recognition and for which service no campaign medal has been awarded. No person in the Navy or Marine Corps can be awarded more than one Expeditionary Medal; however, with the advent of the Armed Forces Expeditionary Medal (p. 98) this latter medal has been issued in lieu of the Navy and Marine Corps Expeditionary Medals for expeditions postdating the issuance of the Armed Forces Expeditionary Medal. Those persons who previously held a Navy or Marine Corps Expeditionary Medal for services other than those for which the Armed Forces Expeditionary Medal has been awarded will be authorized to wear both.

NAVY EXPEDITIONARY MEDAL

Plate 48
(p. 65)
The Navy version of the medal, designed by A. A. Weinman, is $1\frac{1}{4}''$ in diameter and has on its obverse a sailor laboring to bring a landing boat aground. The sailor is armed and in water to his knees. The boat contains armed Marines. Following around the upper edge of the rim is the inscription "EXPEDITIONS." The reverse of the medal has a traditional eagle perched on the shank of a naval anchor, with inscriptions "FOR" and "SERVICE" to the left and right of the eagle, respectively. Branches of what appear to be laurel are entwined about the anchor. "UNITED STATES NAVY" is lettered across the top. The ribbon is yellow and blue.

MARINE CORPS
EXPEDITIONARY MEDAL

Plate 49
(p. 65)

The Marine Corps medal, designed by Walker Hancock, is also 1¼″ in diameter and has on its obverse an advancing Marine equipped with field or battle pack carrying a fixed bayonet on a rifle. In a semicircle at the upper half of the medal is the inscription "EXPEDITIONS." Rippled water is shown in the foreground. The reverse is identical to the Navy medal save for the inscription "UNITED STATES MARINE CORPS." The ribbon is gold and scarlet.

Succeeding expeditions are denoted by bronze stars for both the Navy and Marine Corps medals, although for several years holders of USMC medals wore Arabic numerals on the ribbon to indicate additional expeditions before switching to bronze stars. In addition, Navy and Marine Corps personnel who served in defense of Wake Island from 7 to 22 December 1941, may wear a silver W on the ribbon bar and a clasp inscribed "WAKE ISLAND" on the suspension ribbon.

SECNAVINST 1650.1C is the directive covering this award; authorized by Navy Department General Order No. 84, 15 August 1936.

NC-4 MEDAL

Plate 50
(p. 66)

The NC-4 Medal was created to recognize the extraordinary achievement of members of the NC-4 Flying Boat in making the first successful transatlantic flight in May 1919. The NC-4 was the only surviving aircraft of the three flying boats that started out on this epochal flight. The NC-4 Medal was originally struck as a large gold "table" medal. A bronze miniature of the medal with a suspension ribbon was authorized several years later.

Designed by Catherine G. Barton, the rare medal has on its obverse a gull in flight over waves, with the inscription "FIRST TRANSATLANTIC FLIGHT UNITED STATES NAVY MAY 1919" around the edge. The reverse has an inner circle with "NC-4" in larger lettering, and in smaller letters "NEWFOUNDLAND" and "PORTUGAL" above and below, respectively. In a semicircle at the upper half of the medal are the names of the recipients in raised letters. The recipients are listed as "J. H. TOWERS, A. C. READ, E. F. STONE, W. HINTON, H. C. RODD,

J. L. BREESE, F. RHODES." In the lower half of the medal appears "PRESENTED BY THE PRESIDENT OF THE UNITED STATES IN THE NAME OF CONGRESS." The ribbon is composed of red, white, blue, and green stripes.

Authority was Act of Congress, 9 February 1929.

YANGTZE SERVICE MEDAL

Plate 51
(p. 66)
The Yangtze Service Medal was awarded to members of the Navy and Marine Corps for participation in operations in the Yangtze River Valley, China, between 3 September 1926 and 21 October 1927, and from 1 March 1930 to 31 December 1932. The medal was also awarded to personnel who served ashore at Shanghai. Throughout these dates, a total of 72 ships served in the operation, as well as the Sixth Marine Regiment, Expeditionary Detachment, Aircraft Squadrons, Third Brigade, U.S. Marines of the U.S.S. *Henderson*.

Designed by John R. Sinnock and A. A. Weinman, this handsome $1\frac{1}{4}''$ medal has on the obverse an excellent relief of a Chinese junk at sea. The upper third of the medal has "YANGTZE SERVICE" inscribed. The reverse has a traditional eagle perched on the shank of a naval anchor, with the inscriptions "FOR" and "SERVICE" to the left and right of the eagle, respectively. Branches of what appear to be laurel are entwined about the anchor. This reverse, designed by Weinman, is also used on the Expeditionary Medals of the Navy and Marine Corps, the China Service, Second Nicaraguan, and Dominican Service medals. The ribbon is red, blue, and yellow. Only one medal could be awarded and there are no appurtenances or devices authorized for wear on the medal.

Authority was Navy Department General Order 205, 28 April 1930.

SECOND NICARAGUAN CAMPAIGN MEDAL

Plate 52
(p. 66)
The Second Nicaraguan Campaign Medal was awarded to members of the Navy and Marine Corps for participation in operations in Nicaragua between 27 August 1926 and 2 January 1933. Members of the Army who participated in the Nicaraguan campaigns were also awarded the medal.

This $1\frac{1}{4}''$ medal, struck in unusual clarity and bold relief, is one of the handsomer U.S. service or campaign medals. The obverse, designed by Albert Steward, has as its principal figure Columbia, the poetic feminine symbol of the United States. She is shown with sword at the ready, shielding a female and male figure. Under a linear base are the dates "1926–1930." Almost completely encircling the rim of the medal is the inscription "SECOND NICARAGUAN CAMPAIGN." The reverse is the widely used design of A. A. Weinman found also on five other medals of the Navy Department. The ribbon is bright red with bluish gray stripes. No appurtenances or devices are authorized for wear on this medal.

Authority was Navy Department General Order No. 197, 8 November 1929.

BYRD ANTARCTIC EXPEDITION MEDAL

Plate 53
(p. 67)

The Byrd Antarctic Expedition Medal was intended to express the high admiration in which the Congress and American people held the heroic and undaunted services of members of the Byrd Antarctic Expedition of 1928–30, in connection with the scientific investigations and extraordinary aerial explorations of the Antarctic Continent. The medal was issued to Admiral Byrd in gold, to his officers in silver, and to other personnel in bronze.

Designed by Francis H. Packer, this $1\frac{1}{4}''$ medal portrays on the obverse Admiral Byrd in arctic clothing holding a ski pole, and encircled around the edge of the pendant is the inscription "BYRD ANTARCTIC EXPEDITION 1928-1930." The reverse has a full-rigged sailing ship at the top, and below that on 10 horizontal lines of print are the words "PRESENTED TO THE OFFICERS AND MEN OF THE BYRD ANTARCTIC EXPEDITION TO EXPRESS THE HIGH ADMIRATION IN WHICH THE CONGRESS AND AMERICAN PEOPLE HOLD THEIR HEROIC AND UNDAUNTED SERVICES IN CONNECTION WITH THE SCIENTIFIC INVESTIGATIONS AND EXTRAORDINARY AERIAL EXPLORATION OF THE ANTARCTIC CONTINENT." Below in a head-on view is a relief of a Ford Tri-Motor aircraft used in the Antarctic flights. The ribbon is ice blue and silver white.

Authority was Act of Congress, 23 May 1930.

SECOND
BYRD ANTARCTIC EXPEDITION MEDAL

Plate 54
(p. 67)
The Second Byrd Antarctic Expedition Medal was awarded to deserving personnel of the Second Byrd Antarctic Expedition who spent the winter night at Little America or who commanded either one of the expedition ships throughout the expedition.

Designed by Heinz Warnicke, the $1\frac{1}{4}''$ medal is silver with a white, horizontally grained ribbon bearing no stripes or design. The obverse has the inscription "BYRD ANTARCTIC EXPEDITION" encircled around the edge. In the lower right section are the dates "1933" and "1935." In the center is Admiral Byrd in arctic clothing. An Eskimo dog is to his right, and he has a ski pole in his left hand. The background is representative of the arctic terrain. The reverse has in four sections a Ford Tri-Motor aircraft, a sailing ship, a dog sled and team, and the Little America radio towers. On a square plaque are the words "PRESENTED TO THE OFFICERS AND MEN OF THE SECOND BYRD ANTARCTIC EXPEDITION TO EXPRESS THE VERY HIGH ADMIRATION IN WHICH THE CONGRESS AND THE AMERICAN PEOPLE HOLD THEIR HEROIC AND UNDAUNTED ACCOMPLISHMENTS FOR SCIENCE UNEQUALED IN THE HISTORY OF POLAR EXPLORATION."

Authority was Act of Congress, 2 June 1936.

CHINA SERVICE MEDAL

Plate 55
(p. 67)
The China Service Medal was authorized for award to members of the Navy and Marine Corps for participation during operations in China from 7 July 1937 to 7 September 1939. The medal was again authorized for service in operations in China, Taiwan, and the Matsu Straits from 2 September 1945 through 1 April 1957. When awarded for the post-World War II period, the medal is known as the China Service Medal (Extended).

Personnel who were awarded the CSM for services between 1937 and 1939 and who were again awarded the medal for services since 1945, may wear a bronze star on the ribbon bar and suspension ribbon of the medal to denote a second award. Members of the Army and Air Force who participated in the postwar operations were also awarded the medal by the Navy Department.

The obverse, designed by George H. Snowden, of this $1\frac{1}{4}''$ medal shows a Chinese junk at sea. "CHINA SERVICE" in lettering intended to appear similar to Chinese calligraphic word symbols is imposed above and below the junk. The reverse of the medal is the familiar work of A. A. Weinman. The ribbon of Imperial Chinese Yellow is of silk *moiré* and has a red stripe at each end.

Authority was Navy Department General Order No. 176, 1 July 1942, as amended by ALNAV Instruction No. 25, 22 January 1947 and Navy Department General Order No. 255, 28 January 1948.

UNITED STATES
ANTARCTIC EXPEDITION MEDAL

Plate 56
(p. 68)
The United States Antarctic Expedition Medal was awarded to members of the United States Antartic Expedition of 1939–41 to recognize their valuable services to the nation in the field of polar expedition and science. The *Navy and Marine Corps Awards Manual* states ". . . the Secretary of the Navy is authorized and directed to award gold, silver and bronze medals of appropriate design . . ." The medal illustrated here is of bronze, and it is not known whether gold and silver medals were actually struck and awarded.

Designed by John R. Sinnock, this little-awarded $1\frac{1}{4}''$ medal at first glance bears a strong resemblance to the emblem of the National Geographic Society, having within its circular shape a sharply defined inner circle and map grid lines reminiscent of longitude and latitude markings. Between the outer edge of the medal and the inner circle is the inscription "THE • UNITED • STATES • ANTARCTIC • EXPEDITION" beginning at the lower left of the medal and almost completely encircling the medal. At the bottom are the dates "1939 • 1941." The top half of the inner circle has the inscription "SCIENCE, PIONEERING, EXPLORATION" in a scroll effect. Below this is a grid-lined representation of the polar region inscribed with tiny letters "SOUTH PACIFIC OCEAN, LITTLE AMERICA, PALMERLAND, ANTARCTICA AND SOUTH POLE." The legend "BY ACT OF

CONGRESS OF THE UNITED STATES OF AMERICA TO" is on the upper portion of the reverse, and in the lower portion in extremely fine type is "IN RECOGNITION OF INVALUABLE SERVICE TO THIS NATION BY COURAGEOUS PIONEERING IN POLAR EXPLORATION WHICH RESULTED IN IMPORTANT GEOGRAPHICAL AND SCIENTIFIC DISCOVERIES." The colors of the ribbon, appropriately enough, are ice blue and white.

Authority was Act of Congress, 24 September 1945.

AMERICAN DEFENSE SERVICE MEDAL

Plate 57
(p. 68)

The American Defense Service Medal was awarded for service in the United States Armed Forces for a period of at least one year between 8 September 1939 and 7 December 1941.

The $1\frac{1}{4}''$ pendant was designed by Lee Lawrie, and the silk-*moiré* ribbon, which is $1\frac{3}{8}''$ by $1\frac{3}{8}''$ and is composed of stripes of golden yellow, blue, white, and red with yellow being the prominent color, by Arthur E. Dubois. On the obverse of the medal is a female Grecian figure holding an ancient war shield and brandishing a sword above her head. Around the top are the words "AMERICAN DEFENSE." On the reverse is the wording "FOR SERVICE DURING THE LIMITED EMERGENCY PROCLAIMED BY THE PRESIDENT ON 8 SEPTEMBER 1939 OR DURING THE UNLIMITED EMERGENCY PROCLAIMED BY THE PRESIDENT ON 27 MAY 1941" above a seven-leafed spray.

Army personnel who served outside the continental U.S., including Alaska, are authorized to wear a bronze bar-clasp $\frac{1}{8}''$ wide by $1\frac{1}{2}''$ long on which is inscribed "FOREIGN SERVICE." The clasp has a five-pointed star at each end. Navy and Marine Corps personnel were authorized clasps of a rectangular, rope-edged shape with the inscriptions "FLEET" and "BASE" in block letters, depending on whether they served at sea or at oversea shore bases. The Coast Guard also authorizes a clasp identical to the Navy one, with the inscription "SEA," to show duty differing from their normal offshore based operations. In all services, a bronze star is worn on the ribbon bar to represent possession of a clasp. In addition to the foregoing clasps, Navy, Marine Corps, and Coast Guard personnel who served on certain vessels operating in actual or potential belligerent contact with the Axis forces in the Atlantic Ocean during the period 21 June 1941 to 7 December 1941, are authorized to wear a bronze $\frac{1}{4}''$ letter A. Those wearing the A on the ribbon were not authorized to wear a star concurrently.

Air Force Manual 900-3, Army Regulation 672-5-1, Coast Guard Personnel Manual CG-207, and SECNAVINST 1650.1C are the directives covering this award, authorized by Executive Order No. 8808, 28 June 1941, and promulgated in War Department Bulletin No. 17, 1941, and Navy Department General Order No. 172, 20 April 1942.

AREA CAMPAIGN MEDALS—WORLD WAR II

Creation of the American, the European-African-Middle Eastern, and the Asiatic-Pacific campaign medals were by executive orders. These established initial criteria, described limiting dates and geographical definitions of the respective areas. These executive orders, which ultimately authorized at least one service medal for over nine million service men and women are quoted:

EXECUTIVE ORDER NO. 9265

By virtue of the authority vested in me as President of the United States and as Commander-in-Chief of the Army and Navy of the United States, it is hereby ordered that the American, European-African-Middle Eastern, and Asiatic-Pacific campaign medals, including suitable appurtenances, be established, and that the said medals may be awarded, under such regulations as the Secretary of War and the Secretary of the Navy may severally prescribe to members of the land and naval forces of the United States, including the Women's Auxiliary Corps who, during any period between December 7, 1941, inclusive, and a date six months subsequent to the termination of the present war, shall have served outside the continental limits of the United States in any of the respective areas as indicated by the name of the medals, such areas to be more precisely defined in the regulations hereby authorized.

For purposes of this order, the Territory of Alaska shall be considered as outside the continental limits of the United States.

THE WHITE HOUSE   FRANKLIN D. ROOSEVELT
November 6, 1942

EXECUTIVE ORDER NO. 9706 OF

AMENDING EXECUTIVE ORDER NO. 9265

NOVEMBER 6, 1942, ESTABLISHING

THE AMERICAN, EUROPEAN-AFRICAN-MIDDLE

EASTERN, AND ASIATIC-PACIFIC CAMPAIGN

MEDALS

By virtue of the authority vested in me as President of the United States and as Commander-in-Chief of the Army and Navy of the United States, it is hereby ordered as follows:

1. The European-African-Middle Eastern Campaign Medal shall not be awarded for any service rendered subsequent to November 8, 1945.

2. The American Campaign Medal and the Asiatic-Pacific Campaign Medal shall not be awarded for any service rendered subsequent to March 2, 1946.

3. Effective October 12, 1945, members and former members of the land and naval forces of the United States, including the Women's Reserve of the United States Naval Reserve, and former members of the Women's Army Auxiliary Corps, who served in the continental United States for an aggregate period of one year between December 7, 1941, and March 2, 1946, inclusive, may be awarded the American Campaign Medal under such regulations as the Secretary of War and Secretary of the Navy may severally prescribe.

4. Executive Order No. 9625 of November 6, 1942, establishing the American, European-African-Middle Eastern, and Asiatic-Pacific campaign medals, is amended accordingly.

THE WHITE HOUSE   HARRY S. TRUMAN

March 15, 1946

AMERICAN CAMPAIGN MEDAL

Plate 58
(p. 68)
The American Campaign Medal was awarded for service in the armed forces within the American Theater between 7 December 1941 and 2 March 1946. Conditions for the award were permanent assignment outside the United States, passenger status outside the United States for 30 consecutive or 60 nonconsecutive days, or one year's aggregate service within the continental United States. The area of operations for this medal is shown on the map between pages 88 and 89.

Designed by the Institute of Heraldry, U.S. Army, the medal is of bronze, $1\frac{1}{4}''$ in diameter. On the obverse is a Navy cruiser, a B-24 aircraft flying overhead, and a sinking enemy submarine in the foreground. In the background are some buildings representing the arsenal of democracy, and above this scene the words "AMERICAN CAMPAIGN." On the reverse is an American Bald Eagle between the dates "1941–1945" and the words "UNITED STATES OF AMERICA." The ribbon is of silk *moiré* and is composed of blue, white, black, and red stripes. A bronze star has been authorized for wear on the ribbon by both the Army and the Navy to indicate participation in certain engagements with the enemy. The Army authorized a star for antisubmarine warfare, which was conducted principally by the then Air Corps; the Navy for escort, antisubmarine, armed guard, and special operations.

Air Force Manual 900-3, Army Regulation 672-5-1, Coast Guard Personnel Manual CG-207, and SECNAVINST 1650.1C are the directives covering this award; authorized by Executive Order No. 9265, 6 November 1942 as amended by Executive Order No. 9706, 15 March 1946.

ASIATIC-PACIFIC
CAMPAIGN MEDAL

Plate 59
(p. 69)
The Asiatic-Pacific Campaign Medal was awarded for service in the United States Armed Forces in the Asiatic-Pacific Theater between 7 December 1941 and 2 March 1946. Requirements for the award were permanent assignment, passenger status or temporary duty for 30 consecutive or 60 nonconsecutive days, or combat for which a combat decoration was awarded. A little-known fact is that civilian internees of Japanese prison camps in World War II were also authorized the APCM. This was brought to light in 1963 when I observed a young lieutenant, born in December 1941, wearing the medal. Since the lieutenant would have been only a year old when he earned it, there was considerable doubt in my mind as to his authority to wear such a medal. However, he had been interned at the Santo Thomas Camp from 1942 to 1945 with his mother, and the remote possibility could not be ruled out that he could have been awarded the medal. I

inquired of the Army Adjutant General and he advised me that the lieutenant was indeed authorized the medal as well as the Philippine Liberation Ribbon (p. 162), by virtue of a letter of award issued by the Commanding General, U.S. Army Forces, Far East, dated May 1945. (For area of operation see map between pages 88 and 89.)

Designed by the Institute of Heraldry, U.S. Army, the $1\frac{1}{4}''$ medal has on its obverse a tropical landing scene with battleship, aircraft carrier, submarine, and aircraft in the background, with landing troops and palm trees in the foreground; above this scene the words "ASIATIC-PACIFIC CAMPAIGN." The reverse is the same as that of the American Campaign Medal. The ribbon is of silk *moiré* in orange, white, red, and blue. Devices that may be worn on the ribbon are bronze service stars, silver service stars, and bronze arrowheads.

The same directives and authority as those for the American Campaign Medal apply.

EUROPEAN-AFRICAN-MIDDLE EASTERN CAMPAIGN MEDAL

Plate 60
(p. 69)
The European-African-Middle Eastern Campaign Medal is awarded to personnel of the United States Armed Forces for service in the European-African-Middle Eastern Theater between 7 December 1941 and 8 November 1945. Requirements for the award were permanent assignment, passenger status, or temporary duty for 30 consecutive or 60 nonconsecutive days, or combat for which a combat decoration was awarded. (For area of operation see map between pages 88 and 89.)

Designed by the Institute of Heraldry, U.S. Army, the $1\frac{1}{4}''$ medal has on its obverse an LST landing craft and troops landing under fire, with an aircraft in the background below the words "EUROPEAN-AFRICAN-MIDDLE EASTERN CAMPAIGN." The reverse is the same as that of the American Campaign Medal. The silk-*moiré* ribbon is composed of stripes of brown, green, white, red, black, and blue. Devices that may be worn on the ribbon are bronze service stars, silver service stars, and bronze arrowheads.

The same directives and authority as those for the American Campaign Medal apply.

WOMEN'S ARMY CORPS SERVICE MEDAL
(excluding nurses)

Plate 61
(p. 70)
The Women's Army Corps Service Medal was awarded to women who served in the Women's Army Auxiliary Corps between 20 July 1942 and 31 August 1943 and to those who served in the Women's Army Corps between 1 September 1943 and 2 September 1945. Service in either the Women's Army Auxiliary Corps or the Women's Army Corps is creditable for award of the medal.

Designed by the Institute of Heraldry, U.S. Army, the $1\frac{1}{4}''$ medal is bronze and has on its obverse the head of Pallas Athene superimposed on a sheathed sword crossed with oak leaves and a palm branch within a circle composed of the words "WOMEN'S ARMY CORPS." On the reverse, within an arrangement of 13 stars, is a scroll bearing the words "FOR SERVICE IN THE WOMEN'S ARMY AUXILIARY CORPS" in front of the letters "U.S." Perched on the scroll is an eagle, and at the bottom are the dates "1942–1943." The silk-*moiré* ribbon is in old gold and moss-tone green. No appurtenances or devices are authorized for wear on the medal.

Air Force Manual 900-3 and Army Regulation 672-5-1 are the directives covering this award; authorized by Executive Order No. 9365, 29 July 1943, and promulgated by War Department Bulletin No. 17, 1943; this is the only ribbon or medal specifically created solely for award to female personnel.

WORLD WAR II VICTORY MEDAL

Plate 62
(p. 70)
The World War II Victory Medal was awarded to members of the United States Armed Forces who served for at least one day between 7 December 1941 and 31 December 1946.

Designed by the Institute of Heraldry, U.S. Army, the World War II Victory Medal, like the World War I medal, is 36 mm. in diameter. It has on its obverse a figure of Liberation, right foot resting on a war god's helmet, with the hilt of a broken sword in the right hand and the broken blade in the left, and the words "WORLD WAR II." On the reverse are the words "FREEDOM FROM FEAR AND WANT" and "FREEDOM OF SPEECH AND RELIGION" separated by a palm branch, all within a circle of the words "UNITED STATES OF AMERICA—1941–1945." The silk-*moiré* ribbon is composed of a double rainbow (reminiscent of the World War I VM) in juxtaposition, white stripe, red band, white stripe, and double rainbow in juxtaposition. No clasps, stars, or other devices are authorized for wear with the suspension ribbon or ribbon bar.

Air Force Manual 900-3, Army Regulation 672-5-1, Coast Guard Personnel Manual CG-207, and SECNAVINST 1650.1C are the directives covering this award; authorized by Act of Congress, 9 July 1945 (59 Stat 461).

ARMY OF OCCUPATION MEDAL

Plate 63
(p. 70)
The Army of Occupation Medal was awarded by the Air Force and Army to personnel for service in occupation forces subsequent to World War II. Eligibility for the medal was 30 days' consecutive service in one of the occupation zones listed below within certain time limits.

Austria—9 May 1945 to 27 July 1955

Berlin—9 May 1945 to a termination date to be announced later.

Italy—9 May 1945 to 15 September 1947 (for service in the compartment of Venezia Giulia E Zara or Province of Udine, or with a unit specifically designated in Department of the Army General Order No. 4, 1947).

Japan—3 September 1945 to 27 April 1952 (for service in the main and offshore islands of Japan, plus the Ryukyu Islands and the Bonin-Volcano Islands).

Korea—3 September 1945 to 29 June 1949

NAVY OCCUPATION SERVICE MEDAL

Plate 64
(p. 70)
The Navy Occupation Service Medal was awarded to members of the Navy, Marine Corps, and Coast Guard for service with occupation forces subsequent to World War II. Eligibility for the medal was service with organizations of the Navy during such periods of time when a given organization had been credited by the Secretary of the Navy as having performed duty in one of the occupation zones listed below within certain time limits.

Asiatic-Pacific Area—2 September 1945 to 27 April 1952

European Area—8 May 1945 to 5 May 1955

Italy—8 May 1945 to 15 December 1947

In checking Air Force, Army, and Navy awards regulations, I found that the Navy was far more liberal than the other services in authorizing this award. It appears that personnel in offshore vessels who quite possibly never set foot in an occupied country were awarded the medal en masse. Also interestingly enough, while we never technically occupied Bulgaria, Hungary, or Romania (and the Air Force and Army directives make no mention of these countries) the Navy provides for award of the NOSM to personnel who served in those particular countries.

There were small numbers of personnel in all the services who did not qualify for the occupation medals under the standard criteria, but who, because of participating in the Berlin Airlift, were awarded the Berlin Airlift Device a small gold-colored metal miniature of a C-54 aircraft and, it having been designed to be worn on the occupation medals, the service departments decreed that recipients of the Berlin Airlift Device were also automatically entitled to award of one of the occupation medals.

Although the $1\frac{1}{4}''$ pendants of the occupation medals differ, making them distinct medals, the Air Force, Army, and Navy agreed that regardless of whether a man earned both, only one could be awarded and worn; the selection of which medal a double-recipient wished was left to the individual concerned.

The Army medal, designed by the Institute of Heraldry, U.S. Army, has on its obverse the Remagen Bridge abutments below the words "ARMY OF OCCUPATION." On the reverse is Mt. Fuji, two Japanese sailing vessels, and the date "1945."

The Navy medal, designed by A. A. Weinman, has on its obverse a representation of Neptune—in Roman mythology the god of the sea—mounted, traditional trident in hand, on a composite creature of a charging horse and a sea serpent. Wave scrolls represent the sea and at the bottom and centered within the scrolls is the inscription "OCCUPATION SERVICE." The symbolism of the obverse of the Navy version is rather obscure. The reverse (first seen on the Dominican Campaign Medal [p. 157]) has a traditional eagle perched on the shank of a naval anchor. The inscriptions "FOR" and "SERVICE" appear to the left and right of the eagle, respectively. Branches of what appear to be laurel are entwined about the anchor.

The ribbons of both medals are identical in design, colored white, black, red, and white in that order. The black section of the ribbon is worn to the wearer's right, presumably because Germany, represented by black on the ribbon, surrendered first, thus giving precedence.

There were a total of five clasps authorized for the occupation medals. The only one authorized for wear on the ribbon bar is the Berlin Airlift Device, which was awarded by all services. The other clasps are to be worn on the suspension ribbon only. EUROPE and ASIA clasps, very similar in design to the Navy's World War I ESCORT, FLEET, etc., clasps, are awarded for wear on the Navy medal. The Air Force and Army award clasps are GERMANY and JAPAN, which are similar in design to the Foreign Service clasp authorized for the American Defense Service Medal.

Air Force Manual 900-3 and Army Regulation 672-5-1 are the directives covering the Army medal, authorized by War Department General Order No. 32, 1946. SECNAVINST 1650.1C is the directive covering the Navy medal, which was originally authorized by ALNAV 24, 22 January 1947, and later promulgated by Navy Department General Order No. 255, 28 January 1948.

MEDAL FOR HUMANE ACTION

Plate 65
(p. 71)
The Medal for Humane Action was awarded to personnel assigned to the Berlin Airlift for 120 days or more between 26 June 1948 and 30 September 1949. It also was awarded to persons assigned to units that directly supported the airlift. Persons whose lives were lost while participating in the airlift were awarded the medal posthumously without regard to the 120-day minimum participation period. In a unique decision, the authorities authorized the award of the medal to members of foreign armed forces and to civilians, both U.S. and foreign; however, in these cases, individual recommendations indicating meritorious participation were required.

Designed by the Institute of Heraldry, U.S. Army, the $1\frac{1}{4}''$ medal has on its obverse a facsimile of a C-54 aircraft within a wreath of wheat centered at the bottom of the coat of arms of the city of Berlin. The reverse bears the eagle, shield, and arrows from the seal of the Department of Defense beneath the words "FOR HUMANE ACTION," and above the quotation "TO SUPPLY NECESSITIES OF LIFE TO THE PEOPLE OF BERLIN, GERMANY."

Authority was Act of Congress, 20 July 1949 (65 Stat. 477).

NATIONAL DEFENSE SERVICE MEDAL

Plate 66
(p. 71) The National Defense Service Medal was awarded for any period of honorable service in the United States Armed Forces between 27 June 1950 and 27 July 1954. It also was reinstituted for service between 1 January 1961 and an unspecified terminal date. Reserve forces personnel are excluded from award of the medal except for serving on extended active duty, such as in the case of the activation of their unit, or individual recall to extended active duty. However, should they have earned either the Vietnam Service Medal (p. 100) or Armed Forces Expeditionary Medal (p. 98) during a short call-up period, they are entitled to award of the medal. In addition, service as a cadet or midshipman in the Air Force, Army, or Naval academies during any of the above periods entitles the individual to this medal.

Designed by the Institute of Heraldry, U.S. Army, the $1\frac{1}{4}''$ pendant has on its obverse an eagle displayed with inverted wings standing on a sword and palm branch, all beneath the inscription "NATIONAL DEFENSE." This scene bears a strong resemblance to the pendant designed for the holders of the Certificate of Merit (p. 133). On the reverse is a shield taken from the coat of arms of the United States (paly of 13 pieces of argent and gules; a chief azure), with an open wreath below it. On the right side are oak leaves and on the left laurel. The silk-*moiré* ribbon is composed of stripes of red, white, blue, and yellow.

Persons who earned the medal during the first qualifying period and who again become entitled to the medal wear a device to denote a second award. In the Air Force, Marine Corps, and Navy, a bronze star is worn on the ribbon; in the Army, a bronze oak-leaf cluster.

Air Force Manual 900-3, Army Regulation 672-5-1, Coast Guard Personnel Manual CG-207, and SECNAVINST 1650.1C are the directives covering this award; authorized by Executive Order No. 10488, 1953, as amended by Executive Order No. 11265, 11 January 1966.

KOREAN SERVICE MEDAL

Plate 67
(p. 72) The Korean Service Medal was awarded for service in the Korean Theater between 27 June 1950 and 27 July 1954.

Personnel assigned to Korean operations under any of the following conditions were authorized to wear the award provided they served 30 consecutive or 60 nonconsecutive days or were awarded a combat decoration for a lesser period: assignment in Korea; assignment to a military vessel in Korean waters; assignment to units engaged in aerial missions over Korea; or assignment to units stationed elsewhere that directly supported operations in Korea.

Designed by the Institute of Heraldry, U.S. Army, the $1\frac{1}{4}''$ medal has on its obverse a Korean gateway; encircling the design is the inscription "KOREAN SERVICE." On the reverse is the Korean symbol, *taeguk* (circle), taken from the center of the Korean National Flag, representing the essential unity of all, with the inscription "UNITED STATES OF AMERICA" and a spray of oak and laurel encircling the whole. The ribbon is of United Nations blue and white. Devices that may be worn on the ribbon and medal are bronze and silver service stars, bronze arrowheads, and a miniature Marine Corps device.

Air Force Manual 900-3, Army Regulation 672-5-1, Coast Guard Personnel Manual CG-207, and SECNAVINST 1650.1C are the directives covering the award; authorized by Executive Order No. 10179, 8 November 1950, as amended by Executive Order No. 10429, 17 January 1953.

ANTARCTICA SERVICE MEDAL

Plate 68 (p. 72) The Antarctica Service Medal is awarded to recognize service performed after 1 January 1946 on the Antarctic Continent or in support of U.S. operations there. Persons eligible for this award are members of the United States Armed Forces, or civilian citizens, nationals or resident aliens who participate in scientific, direct support, or exploratory operations on the Antarctic Continent. Included in this group are U.S. Armed Forces aircraft crews flying to and from the continent and U.S. Armed Forces ship crews operating south of latitude 60 degrees south in support of U.S. operations in Antarctica. Citizens of foreign nations may be awarded the medal by special recommendation of the commander of the expedition.

Designed by the U.S. Mint, the $1\frac{1}{4}''$ pendant departs from the much-used ordinary bronze color and is of green-gold colored metal. On the obverse is a view of a polar landscape and the standing figure of a man in Antarctica clothing facing to the front between the horizontally placed inscriptions "ANTARCTICA" on the figure's right, and "SERVICE" to its left. On the reverse is a polar projection with geodesic lines of the continent of Antarctica, across which are the horizontally placed inscriptions "COURAGE," "SACRIFICE," and "DEVOTION," all within a circular decorative border of penguins and marine life. The ribbon is *moiré* silk of black, and graded from a white stripe in the center to a pale blue, light blue, greenish blue, and medium blue.

Air Force Manual 900-3, Army Regulation 672-5-1, Coast Guard Personnel Manual CG-207, and SECNAVINST 1650.1C are the directives covering this award; authorized by Act of Congress, 7 July 1960, as set forth in Public Law 86-600, 86th Congress, and promulgated by Department of Defense Instruction 1348.9, 22 November 1960.

ARMED FORCES EXPEDITIONARY MEDAL

Plate 69
(p. 101)

The Armed Forces Expeditionary Medal may be awarded to any member of the United States Armed Forces who participates in or has participated in military operations for which no other service or campaign medal has been authorized. Primary qualifications for the award are that personnel be attached or assigned to a unit involved in the operation and that he be in the "area of operations" or in "direct support" of the operation for 30 days.

Personnel who earned the AFEM for service in Vietnam prior to 4 July 1965, may exchange it for the Vietnam Service Medal, but once the exchange is made they will not be permitted to revert back to the wearing of the AFEM for Vietnam service.

Campaigns for which the AFEM have been awarded are listed below:

UNITED STATES MILITARY OPERATIONS

Berlin . . . . 14 August 1961 to 1 June 1963
Lebanon . . . . 1 July 1958 to 1 November 1958
Quemoy and Matsu
    Islands . . . . 23 August 1958 to 1 June 1963
Taiwan Straits . . . . 23 August 1958 to 11 January 1959

Cuba ....24 October 1962 to 1 June 1963
Congo................23 November 1964 to
                     27 November 1964
Dominican Republic.....28 April 1965 to 21 September 1966

UNITED STATES OPERATIONS

IN DIRECT SUPPORT

OF THE UNITED NATIONS

Congo................14 July 1960 to 1 September 1962
Korea ....1 October 1966 to a date to be
                     announced

UNITED STATES OPERATIONS

OF ASSISTANCE

FOR FRIENDLY FOREIGN NATIONS

Laos ....19 April 1961 to 7 October 1962
Vietnam .... 1 July 1958 to 3 July 1965
Thailand (in support of
    Vietnam War) .... 1 July 1958 to 3 July 1965

Designed by the Institute of Heraldry, U.S. Army, excellent taste and symbolism were used in designing this beautiful $1\frac{1}{4}''$ bronze medal. On the obverse, superimposed on a radiant compass rose of eight points, is an eagle with wings inverted standing upon a sword loosened in its scabbard, all within the circumscription "ARMED FORCES" above, and "EXPEDI-TIONARY SERVICE" below. On the reverse is the shield from the coat of arms of the United States above laurel branches separated by a bullet, all within the circumscription "UNITED STATES OF AMERICA." The ribbon contains vertical stripes of green, yellow, brown, black, light blue, dark blue, white, and red. Succeeding awards are denoted by bronze stars worn on the ribbon.

Air Force Manual 900-3, Army Regulation 672-5-1, Coast Guard Personnel Manual CG-207, and SECNAVINST 1650.1C are the directives covering this award; authorized by Executive Order No. 10977, 4 December 1961 and Department of Defense Instruction 1348.11, 15 January 1962, as amended 11 July 1962 and 30 January 1963.

VIETNAM SERVICE MEDAL

Plate 70
(p. 101) The Vietnam Service Medal was authorized as an award principally for service in the Republic of Vietnam, contiguous waters off Vietnam, and in Thailand. The latter area accrues entitlement only if the individual was engaged in direct support of operations in Vietnam. The VSM can be awarded to personnel who are on 30 consecutive or 60 nonconsecutive days temporary duty in Vietnam; to permanently assigned personnel for one day in Vietnam; to personnel serving one day aboard a naval vessel in contiguous waters, and also to personnel who serve on one or more flights into Vietnam as an aircraft-crew member in direct support of combat operations.

Personnel previously awarded the Armed Forces Expeditionary Medal for service in Vietnam, may, upon request, exchange that medal for the Vietnam Service Medal; however, no one is authorized to wear both medals solely for service in Vietnam, regardless of the number of occasions for which one may qualify.

Designed by Thomas H. Jones, a sculptor, former employee of the Institute of Heraldry, U.S. Army, the VSM is $1\frac{1}{4}''$ in diameter and has on its obverse a dragon behind a grove of bamboo trees above the words "REPUBLIC OF VIETNAM SERVICE." On the reverse is a crossbow surmounted by a torch above the arched lettering "UNITED STATES OF AMERICA." The ribbon is predominantly yellow, edged in green, with three narrow red stripes in the center. There are several bronze service stars authorized for the various campaigns in the Vietnam War. As of 9 March 1967, there were a total of five declared and additional campaigns with inclusive dates which will be established from time to time.

Air Force Manual 900-3, Army Regulation 672-5-1, Coast Guard Personnel Manual CG-207, and SECNAVINST 1650.1C are the directives for this award; authorized by Executive Order No. 11231, 8 July 1965, and promulgated by Department of Defense Instruction 1348.15, 1 October 1965.

AIR FORCE LONGEVITY SERVICE AWARD

Plate 71
(p. 101) The Air Force Longevity Service Award is awarded to Air Force personnel on active duty who have completed four years' honorable active federal service in any branch of the

83. Coast Guard Expert Rifleman Medal.

84. Coast Guard Expert Pistol Shot Medal.

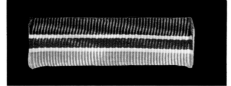

85. Merchant Marine Combat Bar.

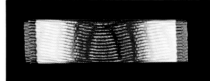

86. Merchant Marine Defense Bar.

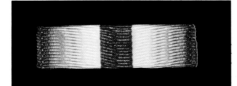

87. Merchant Marine Atlantic War Zone Bar.

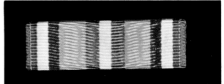

88. Merchant Marine Mediterranean-Middle East War Zone Bar.

89. Merchant Marine Pacific War Zone Bar.

90. Merchant Marine Vietnam Service Bar.

91. Merchant Marine Victory Medal.

U.S. Armed Forces. Service need not be continuous, but must all have been active. This includes active duty for training (annual, special, and school tours) and service as a cadet or midshipman in one of the service academies.

The AFLSA replaces the Federal Service Stripes (hashmarks) formerly worn by enlisted personnel of the Air Force. *Note*: Army regulations prohibit the wear of this award on the Army uniform, since such service in the Army is still indicated by Federal Service Stripes.

The AFLSA is a ribbon of ultramarine blue, divided by four equal stripes of turquoise blue. There is no medal authorized for this ribbon. Succeeding four-year periods of active duty are denoted by bronze and silver oak-leaf clusters.

Air Force Manual 900-3 is the directive covering this award; authorized by Department of the Air Force Special Order No. 60, 25 November 1957.

ARMED FORCES RESERVE MEDAL

Plate 72
(p. 102) The Armed Forces Reserve Medal is awarded to members of the reserve components of the United States Armed Forces who have completed 10 years of honorable and satisfactory service within a 12-year period. Creditable service is defined as service in a non-regular status; however, those persons holding reserve commissions and serving on active duty as warrant officers or enlisted men may credit this concurrent time in computing the 10-year requirement. Service in the following components is creditable toward award of the medal:

Air Force of the United States
Air Force Reserve
Air National Guard
Army of the United States
Coast Guard Reserve
Enlisted Reserve Corps
Marine Corps Reserve
National Guard in the service of the United States
National Guard of the United States
National Naval Volunteers
Naval Militia
Naval Reserve
Officers Reserve Corps
Organized Reserve Corps

Any period during which reserve service is interrupted by one or more of the following will be excluded in computing, but will not be considered as a break in the 12-year period: "During tenure of office by any State official chosen by the voters of the entire State, territory, or possession, or during tenure of office of a member of the legislative body of the United States or of any State, territory, or possession and while serving as judge of a court of record of the United States, or any State, territory, possession, or the District of Columbia."

Designed by the Institute of Heraldry, U.S. Army, the $1\frac{1}{4}''$ medal has on its obverse a flaming torch in front of a crossed powder horn and bugle within a circle composed of 13 stars and 13 rays. The reverse of the medal varies from one component to the other. The Air Force reverse bears an American eagle symbolizing the United States and its air power centered within the words "ARMED FORCES RESERVE" placed around and near the outer rim. The Organized Reserve reverse bears the Minute Man from the Organized Reserve crest on and over a circle of 13 stars centered within the words, "ARMED FORCES RESERVE" placed around and near the outer rim. The National Guard reverse bears the National Guard insignia centered within the words "ARMED FORCES RESERVE" placed around and near the outer rim. The Coast Guard and Marine Corps have their service's insignia centered on the reverse. The Navy has a full-rigged sailing ship coursing, with the standard eagle and naval anchor in the forefront of the ship. The ribbon is of buff and blue. The only device worn on the ribbon is an Hour-Glass with the Roman numeral X superimposed thereon. The Hour-Glass is awarded for 10 years' service after the original award and under the same conditions as prescribed for the first award.

Air Force Manual 900-3, Army Regulation 672-5-1, Coast Guard Personnel Manual CG-207, and SECNAVINST 1650.1C are the directives covering this award; authorized by Executive Order No. 10163, 25 September 1950. (The AFRM has had a history of complex and varied changes in criteria. It was amended by Executive Order No. 10439, 19 March 1953. Some of the legislation involved with this medal are Public Law 810, 80th Congress; Army and Air Force Vitalization and Retirement Equalization Act, 1948; Title III, Section 306c, PL 810, Section 302b [62 Stat. 1087; 10 USC 1036a]; Act of 22 September 1941 [55 Stat. 728; 10 USC 484 note];

and Section 127a, National Defense Act, or Section 515e Officer Personnel Act of 1947 [61 Stat. 906; 10 USC 506d].)

NAVAL RESERVE MEDAL

Plate 73
(p. 102)

The Naval Reserve Medal was established to be awarded to members of the Naval Reserve who had completed 10 years of satisfactory federal service. The entire 10-year period for award must have been spent in reserve components of the Navy will count toward award of the NRM. Service terminating after 12 September 1958 can be accredited only for the Armed Forces Reserve Medal. Navy Department; no service period in the Regular

Designed by the U.S. Mint, the NRM bears on the obverse an American eagle with wings spread grasping a traditional naval anchor in its talons. On the reverse is the circumscription "UNITED-STATES-NAVAL-RESERVE" separated at the bottom by a five-pointed star. In the center appears "FAITHFUL SERVICE." The silk-*moiré* ribbon is red, bordered by narrow stripes of yellow and blue. The ribbon is $1\frac{3}{8}''$ wide and the pendant is $1\frac{3}{8}''$ in diameter. Those who completed a 10-year period of reserve service in addition to that required for award of the basic Naval Reserve Medal could be awarded a bronze star to be worn on the ribbon bar or suspension ribbon.

Navy Personnel Instructions P1615.1C (previously NavPers 15,790 [rev 1953]) is the directive covering this award; authorized by the Secretary of the Navy, 12 September 1938.

ORGANIZED MARINE CORPS RESERVE MEDAL

Plate 74
(p. 102)

The Organized Marine Corps Reserve Medal is awarded to members of the Organized Marine Corps Reserve for four years of service after 1 July 1925. Qualifications for the award are attendance at four annual 14-day field training periods; attendance at 80 per cent of all scheduled drills with an organized unit of the reserve for four years; having received no unsatisfactory fitness reports in the case of officers and, for enlisted men, receiving service record markings of 4.5.

The obverse of this $1\frac{1}{4}''$ medal, designed by John R. Sinnock, shows two figures—a Marine in an old style uniform and a civilian reservist striding together. Around the top is the inscription "MARINE CORPS RESERVE" and at the bottom "FOR SERVICE." The reverse, designed by Maj. Gen. Charles Heywood, USMC, is identical to the Marine Corps Good Conduct Medal (p. 78). The ribbon is red, yellow, blue, and white. Succeeding awards are denoted by bronze stars.

Authority was the Secretary of the Navy, 19 February 1939.

MARINE CORPS RESERVE RIBBON

Plate 75
(p. 103)

The Marine Corps Reserve Ribbon was awarded by the Commandant of the Marine Corps to any member of the Marine Corps Reserve who completed 10 years of honorable service in the reserve. Awards were made during the period 17 December 1945 to 17 December 1965. Regular service and periods of service which were used in computing qualifications for the Organized Marine Corps Reserve Medal may not be counted for this award.

Members of the Marine Corps Reserve who did not serve on active duty in time of war and were members during a war period are not eligible for the award. Marine Corps Reserve service subsequent to 17 December 1965 will be recognized by award of the Armed Forces Reserve Medal.

There is no pendant for this award. The $1\frac{3}{8}''$ ribbon is of the tarnished gold of the Marine Corps with narrow edges of scarlet. Succeeding awards of the ribbon are shown by bronze stars.

AIR FORCE SMALL ARMS
EXPERT MARKSMANSHIP RIBBON

Plate 76
(p. 103)

The Air Force Small Arms Expert Marksmanship Ribbon is awarded by the Air Force for expert marksmanship in small arms. Awarded for firing as "expert" on various small arms, such as pistols, revolvers, carbines, and rifles, it is given only once, regardless of the number of times an individual may qualify.

Designed by the Institute of Heraldry, U.S. Army, the SAEMR is $1\frac{3}{8}''$ wide and has a green center with a wide blue stripe at each edge, with two narrow yellow stripes separating the green and blue. There are no devices to show subsequent requalification, and no pendants for this award.

Air Force Manual 900-3 is the directive covering this award; authorized by the Secretary of the Air Force, 28 August 1962.

AIR FORCE NONCOMMISSIONED OFFICER ACADEMY GRADUATE RIBBON

Plate 77
(p. 103)
The Air Force Noncommissioned Officer Academy Graduate Ribbon is awarded by the Air Force to graduates of accredited Air Force Noncommissioned Officer academies. At these academies senior noncommissioned officers of the Air Force undergo a regimen of training in management, supervisory, public speaking, and military training techniques which is something of a cross between management seminars and a Prussian military school. Upon graduation they are authorized to wear the NOAGR.

Designed by the Institute of Heraldry, U.S. Army, the silk-*moiré* ribbon is predominantly red with a narrow white stripe near each edge and two blue stripes near the center. There is no pendant for this award.

Air Force Manual 900-3 is the directive covering this award; authorized by the Secretary of the Air Force, 28 August 1962.

AIR RESERVE FORCES MERITORIOUS SERVICE RIBBON

Plate 78
(p. 103)
The Air Reserve Forces Meritorious Service Ribbon may be awarded to enlisted members of the Air Reserve Forces for four years of exemplary behavior, efficiency, and fidelity. The first awards were made after 1 April 1965, based on the four continuous years of service immediately preceding the award.

Generally speaking, this is an Air Force Reserve Good Conduct award. Service as a commissioned officer is not creditable toward the qualifying period, nor is service in the reserve components of the Army, Navy, Marine Corps, or Coast Guard.

Designed by the Institute of Heraldry, U.S. Army, the

1⅜″ ribbon is predominantly light blue with white, ultra-marine blue, and yellow stripes at each end. Succeeding awards of the ARFMSR are denoted by oak-leaf clusters. There is no pendant for this award.

Air Force Manual 900-3 is the directive covering this award; authorized by the Secretary of the Air Force, 7 April 1964.

COAST GUARD RESERVE
MERITORIOUS SERVICE RIBBON

Plate 79
(p. 103)

The Coast Guard Reserve Meritorious Service Ribbon is awarded to those members of the Coast Guard Reserve whose service over a four-year period has been marked by excellence in performance and who have met stringent requirements of attendance at drills. Any unfavorable marks in the service record will serve to disqualify an individual for this award. Service performed in regular components of the Coast Guard does not qualify for the award. Second and succeeding awards of the ribbon are marked by $\frac{3}{16}$″ bronze stars.

Established by Secretary of the Treasury, date unknown. Directive is Coast Guard Manual CG207. Award is made only to enlisted men.

NAVY RESERVE
MERITORIOUS SERVICE MEDAL

Plate 80
(p. 103)

The Navy Reserve Meritorious Service Medal is awarded to those Naval Reservists who perform four consecutive years of satisfactory reserve service. Awarded for higher levels of performance than that normally expected of reservists, the medal ranks just below the Naval Reserve Medal in precedence.

The ribbon is 1⅜″ in width and the pendant is 1⅜″ in diameter.

SECNAVINST 1650.1C covers the award; authorized by Secretary of the Navy, 1959.

NAVY EXPERT PISTOL SHOT MEDAL
NAVY EXPERT RIFLEMAN MEDAL

Plates 81, 82
(p. 104)
These medals are awarded upon attainment of rigidly pre-scribed marksmanship requirements established in the Navy Landing Party Manual.

They have ribbons of $1\frac{3}{8}''$ width in Navy Blue with white stripes differentiating between the medals. The Expert Pistol Shot Medal has two white stripes, one at either end of the ribbon and the Expert Rifleman has three, one in the center and two at opposite ends of the ribbon. Pendants are identical except for the inscriptions. Each pendant is a $1\frac{1}{4}''$ circular disk with a smaller disk superimposed at the top to which the pendant is hooked to the ribbon. The smaller disk has a U.S. styled eagle with wings outspread, grasping in its talons the traditional Navy Anchor. The larger disk has a bull's-eye target in raised relief in the center and on the lower edge is the inscription, "UNITED STATES NAVY." Above the target are the words "EXPERT PISTOL SHOT" or "EXPERT RIFLEMAN" as appropriate. The pendants are bronze. Both medals were designed by the U.S. Mint.

COAST GUARD EXPERT RIFLEMAN MEDAL

Plate 83
(p. 105)
The Coast Guard Expert Rifleman Medal, a shield $1\frac{7}{16}''$ high on a $1\frac{3}{8}''$ Navy Blue ribbon, is awarded upon attainment of rigidly prescribed marksmanship requirements established by the Commandant, U.S. Coast Guard. Authorized by the Secretary of Transportation.

COAST GUARD EXPERT PISTOL SHOT MEDAL

Plate 84
(p. 105)
The Coast Guard Expert Pistol Shot Medal, a shield $1\frac{7}{16}''$ high on a $1\frac{3}{8}''$ Navy Blue ribbon, is awarded upon attainment of rigidly prescribed marksmanship requirements established by the Commandant, U.S. Coast Guard. Authorized by the Secretary of Transportation.

MERCHANT MARINE
CAMPAIGN AND SERVICE AWARDS

COMBAT BAR

Plate 85
(p. 106)

The Merchant Marine Combat Bar was awarded to crews of Merchant Marine vessels attacked by hostile forces or suffering damage as a result of enemy action. It was designed by the Headquarters Staff, Maritime Administration, and authorized by Congress on 10 May 1943.

DEFENSE BAR

Plate 86
(p. 106)

The Merchant Marine Defense Bar was awarded to crew members of merchant ships for service between 8 September 1939 and 7 December 1941. It was designed by the Headquarters Staff, Maritime Administration, and authorized by Act of Congress, 10 May 1943.

ATLANTIC WAR ZONE BAR

Plate 87
(p. 106)

The Atlantic War Zone Bar was awarded to personnel who served in the Atlantic War Zone. It was designed by the Headquarters Staff, Maritime Administration, and authorized by Act of Congress, 10 May 1943.

MEDITERRANEAN-MIDDLE EAST
WAR ZONE BAR

Plate 88
(p. 106)

The Mediterranean-Middle East War Zone Bar was awarded to personnel who served aboard ships in the Mediterranean and Middle East. It was designed by the Headquarters Staff, Maritime Administration, and authorized by Act of Congress, 10 May 1943.

PACIFIC WAR ZONE BAR

Plate 89
(p. 106)

The Pacific War Zone Bar was awarded to personnel who served in the Pacific War Zone. It was designed by the Headquarters Staff, Maritime Administration, and authorized by Act of Congress, 10 May 1943.

VIETNAM SERVICE BAR

Plate 90
(p. 106) The Vietnam Service Bar is awarded to personnel for service on U.S. ships serving in waters in and adjacent to Vietnam. It was designed by R. A. Chandler, Maritime Administration, and authorized by Public Law 759, 84th Congress.

VICTORY MEDAL

Plate 91
(p. 106) The Merchant Marine Victory Medal was awarded to personnel who served in the Merchant Marine for 30 days between 7 December 1941 and 3 September 1945. It was designed by John R. Sinnock, U.S. Mint, and authorized by Act of Congress, 8 August 1946.

KOREAN WAR SERVICE BAR

The Korean War Service Bar was awarded to personnel who served on U.S. ships in the Korean War Zone between 30 June 1950 and 30 September 1953. It was designed by the Headquarters Staff, Maritime Administration, and authorized by Public Law 759, 84th Congress.

3

U.S. UNIT AWARDS

Unit awards are made to entire organizations for outstanding heroism or achievement performed during periods of war or international tension. They are not tendered as a means of recognizing single, individual actions, but to cite the combined efforts of every member of an organization in the accomplishment of a common goal.

When, for example, a bomber wing accomplishes spectacular, massive destruction of an enemy target, honor and glory will be heaped upon those brave and skillful men who flew on that particular mission. They will be acclaimed, feted, and decorated for their individual actions on that mission, but also to be credited are the mechanics who maintained the aircraft; the armorers who loaded the bombs and guns; the hospital men who kept the crew members healthy; the cooks who fed them; the supply and administrative personnel who gave them their equipment, handled the paperwork, kept them supplied with properly trained replacements, and assisted in their personal affairs; the Security Police who guarded them and their equipment; and the intelligence men who plotted their mission. Their role is certainly less glamorous but without them the mission could never have taken place. These people and all the others who operate at the first echelon in combat support are recognized by means of unit awards. Thus a person who gave his best at an inconspicuous post and who would not normally be singled out for decoration is rewarded for his part in an outstanding action.

Unit awards are displayed on the uniform by means of the varied insignia on the following pages. The unit itself may indicate possession of an award by the use of streamers (swallowtailed pennants the same color as the personal award) affixed to the unit guidon, by silver bands on the guidon staff or actual decorations attached to guidons, or in the case of the Air Force, by painting the emblem on the unit aircraft. Some unit awards may be worn by persons assigned to the organization after the cited action. These persons may wear the award only as long as they remain in the organization. Those assigned to an organization when it is cited are entitled to wear the award permanently.

All unit awards of one service may be awarded to the other services and may be worn on all service uniforms. Formerly, there was one exception: the Meritorious Unit Commendation (p. 121) awarded by the Army. Regulations of the other services did not provide for the wearing of that insignia (a golden $1\frac{5}{8}''$ laurel wreath on a $2''$ square Army Green shade 44 cloth) on their uniforms; however, since the individual emblem has been changed from a sleeve patch to a device similar to the Army Distinguished Unit Citation, this restraint no longer applies.

PRESIDENTIAL UNIT CITATION

AIR FORCE AND ARMY

Plate 92 (p. 125) The Presidential Unit Citation is awarded by the Air Force and Army to personnel assigned to combat units at the time the unit is awarded a Presidential Unit Citation Award. The individual insignia is called the Presidential Unit Citation Emblem. The Air Force and Army Presidential Unit Citation was officially designated as the "Distinguished Unit Citation" when originally created, but this latter title never really took hold, and the award was commonly spoken of in its present title. Apparently the Air Force and Army capitulated to common usage and in 1965 the terminology was changed.

The PUC is awarded to combat units of the United States and its Allies for extraordinary heroism in action against an armed enemy of the United States, or in action against hostile forces. The degree of heroism required for award to a unit is the same as that which would be required for an individual to be awarded the Distinguished Service Cross (p. 23) or the Air Force Cross (p. 22). Personnel assigned to the unit at the time of the action for which the unit was cited are entitled to wear the emblem permanently. Those who join the organization after the engagement for which the unit was cited are authorized to wear the emblem only as long as they are assigned to that unit.

Designed by Arthur E. Dubois and modeled by Trygve A. Rovelstad, the Army emblem is a blue ribbon $1\frac{3}{8}''$ wide and $\frac{3}{8}''$ high behind a gold-colored $\frac{1}{16}''$ wide metal frame with laurel leaves, and is worn on the right breast over the pocket. The Air Force emblem is essentially the same; however, the frame is smaller so that it will fit in alignment with other ribbons. Air Force, Coast Guard, Marine Corps, and Navy personnel wear the insignia on the left side along with their other ribbons. The British Army, to whose units we have on occasion awarded the PUC, directs that the emblem be worn on the left shoulder in the same location as the British "flash" or unit-designating insignia. Succeeding awards are denoted by bronze oak-leaf clusters.

Air Force Manual 900-3 and Army Regulation 672-5-1 are the directives covering this award; authorized by Executive Order No. 9075, 26 February 1942 (7 Fed. Reg. 1587), as superseded by Executive Order No. 10694, 10 January 1957. (Awards were made for actions occurring on or after 7 December 1941.)

NAVY

Plate 93
(p. 125) The Navy Presidential Unit Citation is awarded by the Secretary of the Navy to units of the United States Navy, Marine Corps, and Coast Guard for outstanding performance in action. The award may also be made to units of the Air Force and Army.

The award is made to units that perform service above and beyond the normal required and in a superior manner when compared with other units performing comparable duties. Personnel assigned to the unit at the time of the action for which the unit was cited are entitled to wear the citation permanently. Individuals who join the unit after the action for which it was cited are authorized to wear the citation only as long as they are assigned to that unit.

The Navy PUC ribbon is very distinctive, having its stripes separated horizontally instead of vertically as is the norm. The colors are blue, gold, and scarlet, with the blue uppermost. Succeeding awards are indicated by bronze stars worn on the gold part of the $1\frac{3}{8}''$ ribbon. Personnel assigned to the

U.S.S. *Nautilus* during the period for which it was awarded the Presidential Unit Citation are authorized to wear a gold N on the emblem. Those aboard the U.S.S. *Triton* when it was cited are authorized to wear a bronze Globe on the citation ribbon.

SECNAVINST 1650.1C is the directive covering this award; authorized by Executive Order No. 9050, 6 February 1942, as amended by the President on 28 June 1943. Navy Department General Order No. 187, 3 February 1943, promulgated the authority. The same Executive Order (No. 10694, 10 January 1957) amending the Air Force and Army awards of the PUC also applies to the Navy award.

VALOROUS UNIT AWARD

Plate 94   The Valorous Unit Award is awarded by the Army to units
(p. 125)   of the United States Armed Forces for extraordinary heroism against an armed enemy in actions on or after 3 August 1963. The award can also be given to cobelligerents of other nations. It is awarded for a lesser degree of gallantry, determination, and *esprit de corps* than that required for the Presidential Unit Citation. The degree of gallantry must be the same as that for an individual to earn the Silver Star Medal (p. 26).

Personnel assigned to the unit during the period for which the unit was commended are entitled to wear the emblem permanently. Individuals who join the organization after the period for which commended are authorized to wear the emblem only as long as they are assigned to that unit. The award will not ordinarily be made to units larger than a brigade or battalion.

Designed by the Institute of Heraldry, U.S. Army, the ribbon is red, white, and blue, banded by a gold frame. Succeeding awards are denoted by bronze oak-leaf clusters.

Army Regulation 672-5-1 is the directive covering this award.

MERITORIOUS UNIT COMMENDATION

NAVY

Plate 95   The Navy Meritorious Unit Commendation is awarded by
(p. 125)   the Secretary of the Navy to units which distinguish them-

selves by outstanding heroism in action against the enemy, or by extremely meritorious service not involving combat but in support of military operations. The degree of heroism or merit for an award to a unit is the same as that which would be required for an individual to receive the Silver Star Medal (p. 26) or Legion of Merit (p. 27), respectively.

Personnel assigned to the unit at the time of the action for which the unit was cited are entitled to wear the $1\frac{3}{8}''$ ribbon permanently. Individuals who join the organization after the service for which the unit was commended may wear the emblem for only the duration of their assignment to that particular unit.

This award, unlike the Navy Presidential Unit Citation, has the standard vertical stripes and is colored green, red, yellow, and blue. Succeeding awards are denoted by bronze stars.

SECNAVINST 1650.1C is the directive covering this award; authorized by the Secretary of the Navy, ALNAV Instructions 224, 18 December 1944.

ARMY

Plate 96 (p. 125) The Army Meritorious Unit Commendation was originally awarded to only Army units and was not authorized for wear by the other services. However, since 1 March 1961, the award can be made to any of the units of the United States Armed Forces or its Allies for exceptionally meritorious conduct in the performance of outstanding service for at least six months in support of military operations.

Personnel assigned to the unit during the period for which the unit was commended are entitled to wear the emblem permanently. Individuals who join the organization after the period for which it was commended are authorized to wear the emblem for only the duration of their assignment to that unit.

Designed by the Institute of Heraldry, U.S. Army, the $1\frac{7}{16}''$ ribbon is identical in design to the Air Force-Army Presidential Unit Citation except that the color of the ribbon is scarlet. Succeeding awards are denoted by bronze oak-leaf clusters.

Army Regulation 672-5-1 is the directive covering this award.

AIR FORCE OUTSTANDING UNIT AWARD

Plate 97
(p. 125)

The Air Force Outstanding Unit Award is awarded by the Air Force to units of the United States Armed Forces who have distinguished themselves by exceptionally meritorious achievement or meritorious service in support of military operations, or service of a great national or international significance when not in support of combat operations. Generally the degree of meritorious achievement for the award to a unit is the same as that which would be required for an individual to be awarded the Legion of Merit (p. 27).

Personnel assigned to the unit at the time of the service for which the unit was cited are entitled to wear the ribbon permanently. Those who join the organization after the engagement for which cited are authorized to wear the ribbon only as long as they are assigned to that unit.

Designed by the Institute of Heraldry, U.S. Army, the $1\frac{3}{8}''$ ribbon is red, white, and blue. Succeeding awards are denoted by bronze oak-leaf clusters.

Air Force Manual 900-3 is the directive covering this award; authorized by the Secretary of the Air Force as announced by Department of the Air Force General Order No. 1, 6 January 1954.

COAST GUARD UNIT
COMMENDATION RIBBON

Plate 98
(p. 125)

The Coast Guard Unit Commendation Ribbon is awarded by the Commandant of the Coast Guard to any ship, aircraft, or other unit which has distinguished itself by extremely meritorious service not involving combat, but in support of Coast Guard operations. The unit must be compared as outstanding when rated with other units performing similar service. It must have performed service as a unit of a character comparable to that which would merit the award of a Coast Guard Commendation Medal (p. 52) to an individual.

Personnel permanently assigned or attached to the commended unit who were present for duty and participated in the cited action are authorized to wear the ribbon permanently. Personnel who join the unit subsequent to the cited period are not authorized to wear the ribbon at any time.

The $1\frac{3}{8}''$ ribbon is identical in color and design to the Navy Meritorious Unit Commendation except that a white stripe appears in the center of the ribbon.

Coast Guard Personnel Manual CG-207 is the directive covering this award; authorized by an approved Board of Awards recommendation, 30 January 1963.

GALLANT SHIP CITATION RIBBON

Plate 99
(p. 126)

The Gallant Ship Citation Ribbon was awarded to Merchant Marine personnel during World War II who served aboard a ship engaged in outstanding action against attack by an enemy, or in gallant action in marine disasters, or other sea emergencies.

Designed by the Headquarters Staff, Maritime Administration, the ribbon is blue with narrow white stripes on each end and has a white miniature sea horse in the center.

It was authorized by Act of Congress, 10 May 1943.

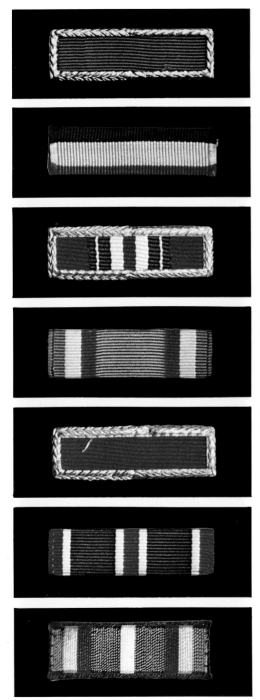

92. Air Force and Army Presidential Unit Citation.

93. Navy Presidential Unit Citation.

94. Valorous Unit Award.

95. Navy Meritorious Unit Commendation.

96. Army Meritorious Unit Commendation.

97. Air Force Outstanding Unit Award.

98. Coast Guard Unit Commendation Ribbon.

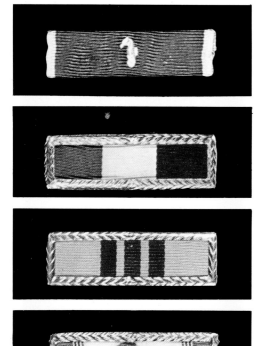

99. Gallant Ship Citation Ribbon.

100. Philippine Presidential Unit Citation Emblem.

101. State of Vietnam Ribbon of Friendship.

102. Korean Presidential Unit Citation Emblem.

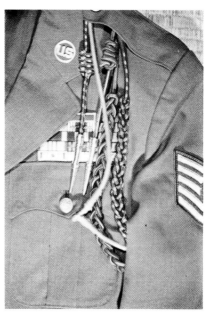

103. Netherlands Orange Lanyard (*left*), French Fourragère (*center*), Belgian Fourragère (*right*).

4

FOREIGN UNIT AWARDS

Qualification for unit awards tendered by foreign governments in recognition of services rendered by United States forces are usually quite similar to those required of U.S. unit awards.

The first of these foreign awards to U.S. units occurred during World War I when the French Government conferred the fourragère to the Croix de Guerre on several units of the American Expeditionary Forces. Later, the Belgian and Netherlands governments followed suit. In World War II the Commonwealth of the Philippines created their unit award, followed in the Korean War by the Republic of Korea. In 1954 the South Vietnam government created the State of Vietnam Ribbon of Friendship which later became widely known as the Republic of Vietnam Presidential Unit Citation and was awarded on a fairly large scale to U.S. forces. Recently, the South Vietnam government instituted a system whereby units could be awarded any of several decorations which are ordinarily considered "personal" decorations, e.g., Cross of Gallantry, etc. When these are awarded to a unit, the decoration is personally awarded to the commanding officer of the unit and the rest of the men of the unit receive the ribbon of the award as a unit award. These Vietnamese personal type decorations, when worn as a unit award, have the ribbon encased in a $\frac{1}{16}$" wide gold frame, as is the case with several other unit awards.

PHILIPPINE PRESIDENTIAL
UNIT CITATION EMBLEM

Plate 100
(p. 126) The Philippine Presidential Unit Citation Emblem was awarded to members of units of the United States Armed Forces for services culminating in the liberation of the Philippine Islands during World War II. The selected units were cited for service between 7 December 1941 and 10 May 1942, inclusive, and from 17 October 1944 to 4 July 1945, inclusive. The conditions of the award were the same as would have been required for award of the United States Presidential Unit Citation. The award was made in the name of the President of the Republic of the Philippines.

The emblem is not authorized for temporary wear by personnel joining an organization after the period for which it was cited. The emblem is worn with the blue portion to the right. The Army wears the emblem in the large size above the right pocket. The other services wear a smaller size to correspond with the other ribbons and sandwich it in with the other ribbons.

The ribbon is of standard width and height with three stripes—blue ($\frac{31}{64}''$), white ($\frac{13}{32}''$), and red ($\frac{31}{64}''$) behind a gold-colored frame ($\frac{1}{16}''$) with laurel leaves. There are no devices which can denote succeeding awards.

Air Force Manual 900-3, Army Regulation 672-5-1, Coast Guard Personnel Manual CG-207, and SECNAVINST 1650.1C are the directives covering this award. Congressional approval is not required.

STATE OF VIETNAM
RIBBON OF FRIENDSHIP

Plate 101
(p. 126) The State of Vietnam Ribbon of Friendship, also known as the Vietnam Presidential Unit Citation, was tendered to the United States Military Assistance Advisory Group in Indochina for services rendered during August and September 1954. It may not be worn by personnel assigned to the group after the cited period.

Designed by personnel of Heraldic Section, Ministry of Armed Forces, Republic of Vietnam, the ribbon is the standard $1\frac{3}{8}''$ wide and $\frac{3}{8}''$ high with stripes of golden yellow ($\frac{7}{16}''$), red ($\frac{1}{8}''$), golden yellow ($\frac{1}{16}''$), red ($\frac{1}{8}''$), golden yellow ($\frac{1}{16}''$), red ($\frac{1}{8}''$), and golden yellow ($\frac{7}{16}''$). The ribbon is behind a gilt frame.

The Army wears the emblem in the large size above the right pocket. The other services wear a smaller size to correspond with other ribbons and sandwich it in with the other ribbons.

Authority was by decree of the Republic of Vietnam, 1954.

KOREAN PRESIDENTIAL
UNIT CITATION EMBLEM

Plate 102
(p. 126) The Korean Presidential Unit Citation Emblem was first awarded to units of the United Nations Command for services in Korea under the same conditions as would be required for an award of the U.S. Presidential Unit Citation. Current criteria remains the same as that applicable during the Korean War. The award is made in the name of the President of the Republic of Korea.

The emblem is not authorized for temporary wear by personnel joining an organization after the period for which it was cited. The emblem is worn with the red part of the *taeguk* (circle) uppermost. The Army wears the emblem in the large size above the right pocket. The other services wear a smaller size to correspond with other ribbons and sandwich it in with the other ribbons.

The ribbon is of standard width and height with vertical stripes of green ($\frac{13}{16}''$), white ($\frac{1}{64}''$), red ($\frac{1}{64}''$), white ($\frac{1}{64}''$), red ($\frac{1}{64}''$), white ($\frac{1}{64}''$), green ($\frac{1}{64}''$), and, in the center, white ($\frac{25}{32}''$), with the pattern repeated in inverse order on the right. In the center is a *taeguk* $\frac{15}{64}''$ in diameter, the curves of the arcs one-half the radius of the disc, red to the top and blue to the bottom. The ribbon is behind a gold-colored frame with laurel leaves $\frac{1}{16}''$ wide. There are no devices which can denote succeeding awards.

Air Force Manual 900-3, Army Regulation 672-5-1, Coast Guard Personnel Manual CG-207, and SECNAVINST 1650.1C are the directives covering this award. Congressional approval is not required to accept foreign unit citations.

NETHERLANDS ORANGE LANYARD

Plate 103
(p. 126)
The Orange Lanyard may be awarded by the Netherlands government when a unit has been cited and awarded the Netherlands Military Order of William. It may also be awarded independently. The award of the Orange Lanyard is not automatic, but must be by ministerial decree of the Netherlands Minister of War.

Personnel assigned or permanently attached to and present for duty with a unit during the action for which an Orange Lanyard was awarded may wear it as a permanent part of the uniform. It is not authorized for temporary wear. Wear of the Lanyard is prescribed by Article 123g of the Clothing Regulations of the Royal Netherlands Army.

The Orange Lanyard is a single orange cord $\frac{1}{4}''$ in diameter and 33″ in length, with a loop at each end and a swivel fastened in one of the loops. The cord is looped over the left shoulder and the swivel is placed in the pocket on the left breast.

Army Regulation 672-5-1 is the only U.S. service directive which mentions this award. The origin of the Orange Lanyard has been lost in antiquity.

FRENCH FOURRAGERE

Plate 103
(p. 126)
The French Fourragère was awarded by the French government to numerous units of the United States Armed Forces during both world wars when those units had been cited twice for the Croix de Guerre or for the Medaille Militaire. Individuals may be authorized the fourragère for being a member of a unit when it received both citations for the Croix de Guerre or Medaille Militaire, but he cannot wear the ribbon of the Croix de Guerre or Medaille Militaire unless he has received an individual citation of the award itself.

Personnel assigned or permanently attached to and present for duty with a unit in the actions for which cited are eligible to wear the decreed fourragère permanently. Personnel later assigned or permanently attached to a unit which has been cited, but who were not present for duty with the unit in the actions, may wear a fourragère only for the period of such assignment or attachment.

The French Fourragère is a single cord braided and knotted

in the colors of the Croix de Guerre (green and red) or of the Medaille Militaire (yellow and green) as appropriate, with a loop at the shoulder and a ferrule of metal at the free end. The overall length is 42″; the braided portion is 26″. Above the ferrule is a loop which is attached to the left shoulder. The fourragère is worn on the left shoulder, the cord passing under the armpit. There are no means whereby additional awards may be denoted.

Originally, the fourragère (fourrage means fodder in French) was a rope used by mounted troops to pick up fodder for the horses. First worn as a belt, it later became a mere ornament looking like a string. Cavalry men used it to attach their shako to their uniform allowing them to retrieve a fallen hat without dismounting. In 1872, wear of the fourragère was suppressed by the French Army. On 21 April 1916, a War Ministry circular authorized the creation of the fourragère, and the Croix de Guerre Fourragère was created in June 1916, with the Medaille Militaire Fourragère following in October 1917. The French Ministry of the Armed Forces advises that there was no single designer of the fourragères—several officers and civilians collectively created the design.

Air Force Manual 900-3 and Army Regulation 672-5-1 are the directives covering this award.

BELGIAN FOURRAGERE

Plate 103
(p. 126)
The Belgian Fourragère may be awarded by the Belgian government when a unit has been cited twice in the Order of the Day of the Belgian Army. Award of the fourragère is not automatic, but must be by specific decree of the Belgian government as follows: for World War I, Royal Decree of 26 October 1918 and 14 July 1919; for World War II, Decree from the Regent on 26 March 1945 and 12 March 1951, and for the Korean War, Royal Decree of 26 March 1953.

Personnel assigned or permanently attached to and present for duty with a unit during both actions for which it was cited may wear the fourragère as a permanent part of the uniform. Personnel who were present in only one action are not authorized to wear the fourragère. It is not authorized for temporary wear by personnel who later join the unit.

The Belgian Fourragère is identical to the French Croix de

Guerre Fourragère except that the colors are reversed—red and green. It is also worn the same way as the French Fourragère.

The usual U.S. service directives cover this award, which dates from the 17th century with only vague legends surrounding its origin.

5

PRE-WORLD WAR I DECORATIONS
AND SERVICE MEDALS

The majority of the decorations and service medals issued by the United States to enlisted men and officers alike since earliest times up to World War I are listed on the following pages. All commonly awarded medals are covered, but a few commemorative medals honoring just one individual or medals of essentially civilian service have been omitted.

CERTIFICATE OF MERIT

Plate 104
(p. 145)

The Certificate of Merit was created to reward distinguished soldiers and was awarded by the Army. For over 50 years, the Certificate of Merit remained exactly that—a certificate, granted by the President. It was not until 1905 that a medal was designed for holders of the certificate. In 1918 the decoration for the Certificate of Merit was made obsolete and from then until 1934, holders could have the obsolete decoration replaced by the Distinguished Service Cross (p. 23). Since 1934, the Distinguished Service Medal has been used to replace the Certificate of Merit Medal.

This, the second award made commonly available, was patterned somewhat similar to the Badge of Military Merit (pp. 17, 57). However, unlike the original intent of the Badge of Military Merit, the Certificate of Merit was first restricted to privates. Officers were never awarded the Certificate of Merit.

133

The Certificate of Merit Medal designed by Francis D. Millet, is $1\frac{1}{4}''$ in diameter and has the national colors of red, white, and blue. The obverse has in its center a traditional eagle facing to the right of the medal, and around the inner ridge is the Latin "VIRTUTIS ET AUDACIAE MONUMENTUM ET PRAEMIUM" (The greatest monument is that of virtue and courage). The reverse of the medal bears the words "UNITED STATES ARMY" around the top, and around the bottom are 13 stars. Within this is a wreath, and in the center the words "FOR MERIT."

Authority was Act of Congress, 3 March 1847.

BREVET MEDAL
(MARINE CORPS)

Plate 105
(p. 145)
The Brevet Medal was uniquely a Marine Corps decoration and one of the most rarely conferred of any decoration. It was awarded exclusively to members of the Marine Corps, although the language of its authorization also extended it to members of the Navy who were holders of Senate confirmed, Presidentially issued brevet commissions during the Civil War, the Spanish-American War, the Boxer Rebellion, the Philippine Insurrection, and the Mexican War. The reasons for the award of the brevet commission and the medal were deemed to be for distinguished service and conduct in the presence of the enemy. Twenty-three officers were awarded the medal.

Designed by Quartermaster Sergeant Joseph A. Burnett, USMC, the pendant is in the shape of a bronze cross pattée $1\frac{5}{8}''$ in diameter. The arms of the cross are joined by a superimposed metal circle bearing around the inner edge the words "UNITED STATES MARINE CORPS," and within a still smaller circle is the inscription "BREVET." The reverse bears the words "FOR DISTINGUISHED CONDUCT" in a circle and, within this the words "IN PRESENCE OF ENEMY" in horizontal lines. The pendant is suspended from the $1\frac{3}{8}''$ ribbon by a small Marine Corps insignia; the ribbon is silk *moiré* of dark red and has 13 white stars in a field.

Authority was Secretary of the Navy, 7 June 1921.

DEWEY MEDAL

Plate 106
(p. 146)
This unique award, popularly known as the Dewey Medal and sometimes as the Manila Bay Medal, commemorates the Battle of Manila Bay. The medal was awarded to personnel who were assigned to one of the following ships on 1 May 1898: the U.S.S. *Olympia,* the U.S.S. *McCulloch* (USRC), the U.S.S. *Concord,* the U.S.S. *Baltimore,* the U.S.S. *Boston,* the U.S.S. *Petrel,* and the U.S.S. *Raleigh.*

Designed by Daniel C. French and manufactured by Tiffany and Company, the Dewey Medal has a somewhat larger pendant than usual and is suspended by a tooled bronze bar from a single link of bronze metal. The link connects the bar and the pendant and gives the impression of a chain. The medal, $1\frac{7}{8}''$ in diameter, of bronze, has on its obverse a striking relief of Commodore Dewey, later to become an admiral. Staggered around both sides of the obverse are the words "THE GIFT OF THE PEOPLE OF THE UNITED STATES TO THE OFFICERS AND MEN OF THE ASIATIC SQUADRON UNDER THE COMMAND OF COMMODORE GEORGE DEWEY." Toward the bottom right of the medal is a wreath with an anchor imposed thereon, and below that a dimpled star. The reverse bears a superbly wrought representation of a sailor seated on a naval cannon and holding a flag. Around the edge of the medal are the words "IN MEMORY OF THE VICTORY OF MANILA BAY, MAY 1, 1898." At the bottom is a small panel bearing the name of the ship on which the medal was earned. The ribbon of blue and gold is of heavy grosgrain and is placed behind the pendant, link, and bar.

Authority was Act of Congress, 3 June 1898.

SPECIALLY MERITORIOUS MEDAL

Plate 107
(p. 146)
The Specially Meritorious Medal was seldom awarded. It was created to recognize acts of specially meritorious service, other than in battle, during the war with Spain. There seems to be some doubt as to whether this particular medal should be titled the "Specially Meritorious Medal" or the "Meritorious Service Medal." However, the 1953 edition of the *Navy and Marine Corps Awards Manual* describes it as the former.

The pendant is a strictly defined bronze cross pattée $1\frac{1}{4}''$ in diameter with the arms of the cross having imposed on them in the center a circle of bronze bearing the inscription "U.S. NAVAL CAMPAIGN WEST INDIES," and within the inscription is a wreath of laurel and oak. Within the wreath is a naval anchor. On the four arms of the cross, starting from the left clockwise is the inscription "SPECIALLY MERITORIOUS SERVICE 1898." The reverse is bare. The $1\frac{3}{8}''$ ribbon is of bright scarlet silk *moiré* without pattern or design. Personnel who qualified for the award a second time were presented with an inscribed bronze bar to be attached to the suspension ribbon.

Authority was Act of Congress, 3 March 1901.

CIVIL WAR CAMPAIGN MEDAL

Authorized for Civil War service in the Union Forces, the Civil War medals were not created until 1907 by the War Department and 1908 by the Navy Department. Service recognized was from 15 April 1861 to 9 April 1865, and for an additional period until 20 August 1866 for service in Texas.

ARMY

Plate 108
(p. 146)
Designed by Francis D. Millet, the Army Civil War Campaign Medal pendant is a $1\frac{1}{4}''$ bronze medal. On the obverse is the head of Lincoln surrounded by the words "WITH MALICE TOWARD NONE, WITH CHARITY FOR ALL." On the reverse are the words "THE CIVIL WAR" and the dates "1861–1865" surrounded by a wreath formed by a branch of oak on the left and a branch of olive on the right. The medal is suspended by a ring from a silk-*moiré* ribbon of equal bands of red and gray.

Authority was War Department General Order No. 12, 1907.

NAVY

Plate 109
(p. 147)
Designed by Bailey, Banks and Biddle, the Navy Civil War Medal pendant, also $1\frac{1}{4}''$ in diameter, has on its obverse in vivid relief the battle of the ironclad battleships, the U.S.S. *Monitor* and the Confederate *Merrimac*. The reverse bears an eagle with opened wings astride a naval anchor with affixed chain. Below is the inscription "FOR SERVICE" and at the bot-

tom are oak and laurel branches. At the top is the inscription "UNITED STATES NAVY" (or UNITED STATES MARINE CORPS). The ribbon is blue and gray.

Authority was Navy Department Special Orders 81 and 82, 1908.

INDIAN CAMPAIGN MEDAL

Plate 110
(p. 147)
The Indian Campaign Medal commemorated the 32 years of campaigns and battles against hostile American Indian tribes in the Southwest and Far West of the United States. These campaigns were conducted in Southern Oregon, Idaho, California, and Nevada between 1865 and 1868; against the Comanches and confederate tribes in Kansas, Colorado, Texas, New Mexico, and the Indian Territory between 1867 and 1875; the Modoc War of 1872–73; against the Apaches in Arizona in 1873; against the Northern Cheyennes and Sioux in 1876–77; the Nez Percé War in 1877; the Bannock War in 1878; against the Northern Cheyennes in 1878–79; against the Sheep Eaters, Paiutes, and Bannocks from June to October, 1879; against the Utes in Colorado and Utah between September 1879 and November 1880; against the Apaches in Arizona and New Mexico in 1885–86; against the Sioux in South Dakota between November 1890 and January 1891; and against hostile Indians in unspecified actions up to 1898.

Designed by Francis D. Millet, the pendant is of bronze and is $1\frac{1}{4}''$ in diameter. On the obverse is a mounted Indian carrying a spear in his right hand. Above him in a circle are the words "INDIAN WARS," and below, on either side of a buffalo skull, the circle is completed by arrowheads. In designing the reverse, the designer must have had instructions to produce a design that would serve the several medals recently authorized. It is a mélange of a trophy, composed of an eagle perched on a cannon supported by crossed flags, rifles, an Indian shield, spear and quiver of arrows, a Cuban machete, and a Sulu kris. Below the trophy are the words "FOR SERVICE." The whole is surrounded by a circle composed of the words "UNITED STATES ARMY" in the upper half and 13 stars in the lower. The medal is suspended by a ring from a silk-*moiré* ribbon of red and black.

Army Regulation 672-5-1 covers this award; authorized by War Department General Order No. 12, 1907.

WEST INDIES
NAVAL CAMPAIGN MEDAL, 1898

Plate 111
(p. 148)

The West Indies Naval Campaign Medal was created to commemorate naval and other engagements in the waters of the West Indies and on the shores of Cuba during the war with Spain from 27 April to 14 August 1898. The medal was awarded by the Secretary of the Navy to members of the Navy and Marine Corps whose services during these engagements were of unusual merit. The medal is widely known as the "Sampson Medal" and is even so described in the 1953 edition of the *Navy and Marine Corps Awards Manual*.

The obverse of the $1\frac{1}{4}''$ pendant, designed by Charles E. Barber, bears a bust of Admiral William T. Sampson, with the inscription "U.S. NAVAL CAMPAIGN WEST INDIES 1898" around the upper half of the medal. To the left appears the name "WILLIAM T. SAMPSON," with the "T" barely discernible. To the right of the bust are the words "COMMANDER IN CHIEF." The reverse, designed by George T. Morgan, shows three men—a naval officer, a naval gunner, and on the right a Marine with arms at the ready. Below them is a panel on which names and dates of engagements were inscribed. The silk-*moiré* ribbon is red and blue. A bronze bar was worn at the top of the suspension ribbon bearing the name of the ship on which the man served. Bronze stars were worn on the ribbon to show engagements.

Authority was Act of Congress, 3 March 1901.

CHINA CAMPAIGN MEDAL (ARMY)

Plate 112
(p. 148)

The China Campaign Medal of the Army was awarded to personnel who served ashore in China between 20 June 1900 and 27 May 1901.

Designed by Francis D. Millet, the $1\frac{1}{4}''$ pendant has on its obverse a striking relief of the Imperial Dragon of China within the inscription "CHINA RELIEF EXPEDITION 1900–1901." The reverse is identical to that of the Indian Campaign Medal (p. 137). The ribbon is yellow, edged in blue. Owing to the precedent set by previous awards and decorations authorized by the government, the Boxer Rebellion awards of the Army and Navy have the same ribbon.

Authority was War Department General Order No. 5, 1905.

CHINA RELIEF EXPEDITION MEDAL (NAVY)

Plate 113
(p. 148)

The China Relief Expedition Medal was awarded to personnel who served on shore in China with the Peking Relief Expedition between 24 May 1900 and 27 May 1901. Personnel on the naval vessels U.S.S. *Brooklyn*, U.S.S. *Buffalo*, U.S.S. *Iris*, U.S.S. *Monocacy*, U.S.S. *Nashville*, U.S.S. *New Orleans*, U.S.S. *Newark*, U.S.S. *Solace*, U.S.S. *Wheeling*, U.S.S. *Yorktown*, or U.S.S. *Zafiro* were also awarded the Navy medal.

Designed by Bailey, Banks and Biddle, the Navy medal, also $1\frac{1}{4}''$ in diameter, has on its obverse the inscription "CHINA RELIEF EXPEDITION" encircled around the inner rim and at the bottom "1900." The reverse is the same as the Navy Cuban Pacification Medal (p. 143).

Authority was Navy Department Special Orders 81 and 82, 27 June 1908.

PHILIPPINE CONGRESSIONAL MEDAL

Plate 114
(p. 149)

The Philippine Congressional Medal was awarded by the Army to soldiers who, having entered the service between 21 April 1898 and 26 October 1898, served past their discharge date and who were ashore in the Philippine Islands between 4 February 1899 and 4 July 1902.

Designed by Francis D. Millet, the bronze $1\frac{1}{4}''$ pendant has on its obverse a group composed of a color bearer holding a flag of the United States and two men with rifles between the words "PHILIPPINE" and "INSURRECTION." Below the group is the date "1899." On the reverse are the words "FOR PATRIOTISM, FORTITUDE AND LOYALTY" in a wreath composed of a branch of pine on the left and a branch of palm on the right. The medal is suspended by a ring from a silk-*moiré* ribbon of blue, red, and white.

Army Regulation 672-5-1 covers this award; authorized by Act of Congress, 29 June 1906 (34 Stat. 621).

PHILIPPINE CAMPAIGN MEDAL

The Philippine Campaign Medal was issued by both the Army and Navy. The Army awarded it to soldiers who served in the Philippine Islands against hostile natives between 4 February 1899 and 31 December 1913. The Navy awarded it to naval personnel who served on shore in the Philippine Islands between 4 February 1899 and 4 July 1902 or on shore in Nundanoa, cooperating with the Army between 4 February 1898 and 31 December 1904. Personnel serving on certain vessels in the area were also authorized to wear the medal.

ARMY

Plate 115
(p. 149)
Designed by Francis D. Millet, the Army medal is a bronze $1\frac{1}{4}''$ pendant. On the obverse is a coconut-palm tree. To the left is the lamp of knowledge, and on the right the scales of justice. The whole is in a circle composed of the words "PHILIPPINE INSURRECTION," and the date "1899." The reverse is identical to that of the Indian Campaign Medal (p. 137). The ribbon of both the Army and Navy medals is predominantly blue with wide red stripes.

Authority was War Department General Order 5, 1905.

NAVY

Plate 116
(p. 150)
Designed by Bailey, Banks and Biddle, the Navy medal, also $1\frac{1}{4}''$ in diameter, bears the inscription "PHILIPPINE CAMPAIGN" around the upper half and "1899–1903" at the bottom. Laurel branches separate the words and numerals. Within the inscriptions is an old gateway in the ancient barrio of Manila. The reverse is the same as that of the Navy Cuban Pacification Medal (p. 143).

Authority was Navy Department Special Orders 81 and 82, 27 June 1908.

ARMY OF PUERTO RICO OCCUPATION MEDAL

Plate 117
(p. 150)
The Army of Puerto Rico Occupation Medal was awarded to personnel who served in Puerto Rico between 14 August 1898 and 10 December 1898.

Designed by the Institute of Heraldry, U.S. Army, the pendant is a $1\frac{1}{4}''$ bronze medal. On the obverse is a castle within a circle composed of the words "ARMY OF OCCUPATION, PORTO RICO" in the upper half and the date "1898" at the bottom, with a branch of the tobacco plant on the left and a stalk of sugar cane on the right. The reverse is identical to that of the Indian Campaign Medal (p. 137). The medal is suspended by a ring from a silk-*moiré* ribbon of red, blue, and yellow.

Army Regulation 672-5-1 is the directive covering this award; authorized by War Department Compilation of Orders, change No. 15, 4 February 1919.

ARMY OF CUBA OCCUPATION MEDAL

Plate 118
(p. 150)

The Army of Cuba Occupation Medal was awarded to United States Army personnel who served with occupation forces in Cuba between 18 July 1898 and 20 May 1902.

Designed by the Institute of Heraldry, U.S. Army, the medal of bronze is $1\frac{1}{4}''$ in diameter. On the obverse is the coat of arms of the Cuban Republic with wreath and fasces. Around the circumference are the words "ARMY OF OCCUPATION, MILITARY GOVERNMENT OF CUBA," and the dates "1898" and "1902." The reverse is identical to that of the Indian Campaign Medal (p. 137). The medal is suspended by a silk-*moiré* ribbon of blue, yellow, and red.

Army Regulation 672-5-1 is the directive covering this award; authorized by War Department General Order No. 40, 1915.

SPANISH WAR SERVICE MEDAL

Plate 119
(p. 151)

The Spanish War Service Medal was awarded by the Army for service between 20 April 1898 and 11 April 1899 for personnel not eligible for award of the Spanish Campaign Medal.

The obverse, designed by Colonel J. R. M. Taylor, bears a sheathed Roman sword hanging on a tablet on which is inscribed "FOR SERVICE IN THE SPANISH WAR." The tablet is surrounded by a wreath. The reverse of the $1\frac{1}{4}''$ medal, designed by Bailey, Banks and Biddle, bears a coat of arms of the United States with a scroll below, all surrounded by a wreath displaying the insignia of the Infantry, Artillery, and Cavalry. The medal is suspended by a ring from a silk-*moiré* ribbon of green and yellow.

Army Regulation 672-5-1 is the directive covering this award; authorized by Act of Congress, 9 July 1918 (40 Stat. 873).

WEST INDIES CAMPAIGN MEDAL

Plate 120
(p. 151)

The West Indies Campaign Medal is little-known and was rarely issued. It was struck in limited numbers for award to Navy and Marine Corps personnel for service aboard ships in the West Indies. However, since most of the personnel assigned to these ships had also qualified for the "Sampson Medal" (p. 138), there was little need for the issue of the West Indies Campaign Medal and its use was quickly discontinued.

Designed by Bailey, Banks and Biddle, the $1\frac{1}{4}''$ medal has on its obverse the same scene as that of the Navy version of the Spanish Campaign Medal (p. 143), except for the rimmed space of the inner circle, which bears the inscription "WEST INDIES CAMPAIGN." The ribbon is yellow and blue.

SPANISH CAMPAIGN MEDAL

The Spanish Campaign Medal, awarded by both the Army and Navy for the short-lived war with Spain, bears the same ribbon for both services but, as was often the case early in the 20th century, pendants differed.

ARMY

Plate 121
(p. 151)

The Army awarded the medal to personnel for service in Cuba from 11 May 1898 to 17 July 1898; in Puerto Rico between 24 July 1898 and 13 August 1898; and in the Philippine Islands from 30 June 1898 to 13 August 1898.

Designed by Francis D. Millet, the Army pendant is the usual bronze medal $1\frac{1}{4}''$ in diameter. On the obverse is a castle within a circle composed of the words "WAR WITH SPAIN" in the upper half and the date "1898" at the bottom, with a branch of the tobacco plant on the left and a stalk of sugar cane on the right. The reverse is identical to that of the Indian Campaign Medal (p. 137). The medal is suspended by a ring from a silk-*moiré* ribbon of yellow and blue.

Authority was War Department General Order No. 5, 1905.

NAVY

Plate 122
(p. 152)
The Navy awarded the medal to personnel who served in the Navy between 20 April 1898 and 10 December 1898 aboard ships or ashore in Cuba, Puerto Rico, Guam, or the Philippines.

Designed by Bailey, Banks and Biddle, the Navy pendant is also bronze and $1\frac{1}{4}''$ in diameter. On the obverse in a circle around the inner rim are the words "SPANISH CAMPAIGN" and the date "1898." In the center in excellent relief is Morro Castle of Cuba. A stack of cannon balls is in the foreground. The reverse side is the same as the Navy Cuban Pacification Medal.

Authority was Navy Department Special Orders 81 and 82, 27 June 1908.

ARMY OF CUBAN PACIFICATION MEDAL

Plate 123
(p. 152)
The Army of Cuban Pacification Medal was awarded to soldiers who served in Cuba between 6 October 1906 and 1 April 1909.

Designed by the Institute of Heraldry, U.S. Army, the bronze $1\frac{1}{4}''$ pendant has on its obverse the coat of arms of the Cuban Republic and two American soldiers dressed in the uniform of that era. Above the group are the words "CUBAN PACIFICATION" and below are the dates "1906–1909." The reverse is identical to that of the Indian Campaign Medal (p. 137). The ribbon is red, white, blue, and olive-drab.

Authority was War Department General Order No. 96, 1909.

NAVY CUBAN PACIFICATION MEDAL

Plate 124
(p. 152)
The Navy Cuban Pacification Medal was awarded to personnel who served ashore between 12 September 1906 and 1

April 1909, or who were attached to certain ships within these dates.

Designed by Bailey, Banks and Biddle, the bronze $1\frac{1}{4}''$ pendant has on its obverse the traditional representation of Columbia wearing a sword in scabbard. She is holding a flag with staff in her left hand and an olive branch in her right. A Cuban is kneeling before her. The inscription "CUBAN PACIFICATION 1908" rims the top half of the medal, and a bird, presumably a dove, is in flight. The reverse bears an eagle with opened wings astride a naval anchor with affixed chain. Below is the inscription "FOR SERVICE" and at the bottom are oak and laurel branches. The top of the reverse also bears the inscription "UNITED STATES NAVY" (or UNITED STATES MARINE CORPS). The ribbon is the same as that of the Army of Cuban Pacification Medal.

Authority was Navy Department General Order No. 30, 13 August 1909.

NICARAGUAN CAMPAIGN MEDAL

Plate 125
(p. 153) The Nicaraguan Campaign Medal was awarded to personnel of the Navy and Marine Corps who served in Nicaragua, or on board certain ships between 29 July 1912 and 14 November 1912. The ships were the U.S.S. *Annapolis,* the U.S.S. *California,* the U.S.S. *Cleveland,* the U.S.S. *Colorado,* the U.S.S. *Denver,* the U.S.S. *Glacier,* the U.S.S. *Maryland,* and the U.S.S. *Tacoma.*

Designed by Bailey, Banks and Biddle, the $1\frac{1}{4}''$ pendant is suspended from a silk-*moiré* ribbon of dark red with Navy Blue stripes. On the obverse are the words "NICARAGUAN CAMPAIGN" and the date "1912" around the inner edge. Within that is a rain forest flanking Lake Managua on both sides. In the background is Mt. Momotombo volcano. The reverse has an eagle with spread wings astride a naval anchor with affixed chain. Below is the inscription "FOR SERVICE" and at the bottom are oak and laurel branches. The top of the reverse also has the inscription "UNITED STATES NAVY" (or UNITED STATES MARINE CORPS).

Authority was by Presidential Order on 22 September 1913.

119 (*front & reverse*). Spanish War Service Medal.

120. West Indies Campaign Medal.

121 (*front & reverse*). Army Spanish Campaign Medal.

122. Navy Spanish Campaign Medal.

123 (*front & reverse*). Army of Cuban Pacification Medal.

124. Navy Cuban Pacification Medal.

125. Nicaraguan Campaign Medal.

126. Haitian Campaign Medal.

127. Dominican Campaign Medal.

153

128 (*front & reverse*). Army Mexican Service Medal.

129. Navy and Marine Corps Mexican Service Medal.

130. Mexican Border Service Medal.

131. Peary Polar Expedition Medal (1908–1909).

132. Philippine Defense Ribbon.

133. Philippine Liberation Ribbon.

134. Philippine Independence Ribbon.

135. United Nations Service Medal.

136. United Nations Service Medal with Korean inscription.

137. United Nations Medal.

138, 139. Republic of Vietnam Campaign Medal (*right*) The same medal as worn on mess dress (*far right*).

HAITIAN CAMPAIGN MEDAL

Plate 126
(p. 153) The Haitian Campaign Medal was awarded to Navy and Marine Corps personnel who served in Haiti between 9 July 1915 and 6 December 1915, or who were assigned or attached to ships assigned to the Haitian Campaign. It was also issued to Navy and Marine Corps personnel who served in Haiti between 1 April 1919 and 15 June 1920, or who were assigned to ships that were assigned to Haitian Operations. The second award of this medal was designated by a bar inscribed "1919–1920," when an individual first had earned it in 1915–16. While there was only one basic design for the medal, those who earned it for 1915–16 operations were issued a medal that had the dates "1915–1916" inscribed on the bottom of the obverse, and those issued the medal for 1919–20 operations had "1919–1920" inscribed on the medal.

Designed by Bailey, Banks and Biddle the 1¼″ pendant has on its obverse in a semicircle the inscription "HAITIAN CAMPAIGN." In the left foreground is a tropical palm, and in the background are waves, a shoreline, and mountains. The reverse has an eagle with opened wings astride a naval anchor with affixed chain. Below is the inscription "FOR SERVICE" and at the bottom are oak and laurel branches. The top of the reverse has the inscription "UNITED STATES NAVY" (or UNITED STATES MARINE CORPS). The ribbon is of deep blue with narrow stripes of red in the center.

Authority was Navy Department General Order No. 305, 22 June 1917.

DOMINICAN CAMPAIGN MEDAL

Plate 127
(p. 153) The Dominican Campaign Medal was awarded to Navy and Marine Corps personnel who served in operations in Santo Domingo in 1916. Inclusive dates for the award for personnel who participated in the campaign were 5 May 1916 to 4 December 1916.

Designed by A. A. Weinman, the 1¼″ bronze pendant has a very narrow rim with the "Tower of Homage" in Ciudad Trujillo shown in bas-relief. In the foreground are breaking waves and a seawall. The reverse of the medal has a traditional eagle perched on the shank of a naval anchor with the inscriptions "FOR" and "SERVICE" to the left and right, respectively, of the eagle. Branches of what appear to be laurel are entwined about the anchor. The ribbon is crimson with two blue stripes in the center.

Authority was Navy Department General Order No. 76, 19 December 1921.

MEXICAN SERVICE MEDAL

The Mexican Service Medal was awarded to Army, Navy, and Marine Corps personnel who served against hostile Mexicans between 12 April 1911 and 7 February 1917, or who fought in one of the following engagements: Buena Vista, Mexico, on 1 December 1917; San Bernardino Canon, Mexico, on 26 December 1917; La Grulla, Texas, on 8 and 9 January 1918; Pilares, Mexico, on 28 March 1918; Nogales, Arizona, 1 through 5 November 1915 or 27 August 1918; El Paso, Texas, and Jaurez, Mexico, on 15 and 16 June 1919; and Vera Cruz Expedition from 21 to 23 April 1914.

ARMY

Plate 128
(p. 154)

Designed by Colonel J. R. M. Taylor, the Army medal is of bronze $1\frac{1}{4}''$ in diameter and has on its obverse a Mexican yucca plant in flower, with mountains in the background. Above the yucca plant are the words "MEXICAN SERVICE" and in the lower half the dates "1911–1917." The reverse is a trophy composed of an eagle perched on a cannon supported by crossed flags, rifles, an Indian shield, spear and quiver of arrows, a Cuban machete, and a Sulu kris. Below the trophy are the words "FOR SERVICE." The whole is surrounded by a circle composed of the words "UNITED STATES ARMY" in the upper half and 13 stars in the lower. The medal is suspended by a ring from a silk-*moiré* ribbon of green, yellow, and blue.

Authority was War Department General Order No. 155, 1917.

NAVY

Plate 129
(p. 154)

Designed by Bailey, Banks and Biddle, the Navy and Marine Corps pendant is a more clearly wrought medal than the

Army version, and has on its obverse the inscription "MEXICO" and the dates "1911–1917" in bold face; within an inner circle is a castle in Veracruz harbor. On either side of the castle within the circle appear what may be cacti. The reverse is the same as the Haitian Campaign Medal (p. 157). The ribbon is the same as for the Army medal.

Authority was Navy Department General Order No. 365, 11 February 1918.

MEXICAN BORDER SERVICE MEDAL

Plate 130
(p. 154) The Mexican Border Service Medal was awarded to Army personnel for service between 9 May 1916 and 24 March 1917, or for those who served with the Mexican Border Patrol between 1 January 1916 and 6 April 1917 who were not eligible for the Mexican Service Medal.

Designed by Colonel J. R. M. Taylor, the $1\frac{1}{4}''$ bronze pendant has on its obverse a sheathed Roman sword hanging on a tablet on which is inscribed "FOR SERVICE ON THE MEXICAN BORDER." The reverse is the same as that of the Spanish War Service Medal (p. 141). The ribbon is of silk *moiré,* colored green and yellow.

Authority was Act of Congress, 9 July 1918 (40 Stat. 873).

PEARY POLAR EXPEDITION MEDAL (1908-9)

Plate 131
(p. 155) The Peary Polar Expedition Medal (1908–9) was created to commemorate certain members of the Peary Polar Expedition of 1908–9 for their service in the field of science and for the causes of polar exploration by aiding in the discovery of the North Pole by Admiral Robert E. Peary.

Designed by John R. Sinnock, under direction of the Secretary of the Navy, the $1\frac{1}{4}''$ pendant is silver with a predominantly ivory-colored ribbon with turquoise stripes. On the obverse of the medal is Admiral Peary holding what might be a ski pole in his right hand. In three horizontal lines in descending-size type is the inscription "PEARY POLAR EXPEDITION 1908–09." Around the inner rim of the medal are the 15 points of a compass rose. The top centered point is replaced by a fleur-de-lis. The reverse has in its top third an unfurled American flag with 46 stars, flanked by two Eskimo dogs. Below are the words "PRESENTED IN THE NAME OF CONGRESS IN RECOGNITION OF HIS EFFORTS AND SERVICES AS A MEMBER OF THE PEARY POLAR EXPEDITION OF 1908–1909 IN THE FIELD OF SCIENCE AND FOR THE CAUSE OF POLAR EXPLORATION BY AIDING IN THE DISCOVERY OF THE NORTH POLE BY ADMIRAL PEARY." In the bottom third s a blank area for engraving the recipient's name. At the very bottom are a pair of minute snowshoes.

Authority was Act of Congress, 28 January 1944.

6

SERVICE MEDALS AWARDED TO U.S. FORCES BY FOREIGN GOVERNMENTS

Although there are six medals discussed here, only one can be truly classified as being awarded by a "foreign" government —the Republic of Vietnam Campaign Medal. The three Philippine awards were created and authorized by the Commonwealth of the Philippines which was then administratively a part of the United States, and, of course the United Nations awards are exclusively of that organization. However, since all stem from entities other than the United States government, they are placed in the very general classification of awards of foreign governments.

PHILIPPINE DEFENSE RIBBON

Plate 132
(p. 155)
The Philippine Defense Ribbon was awarded to personnel who participated in the defense of the Philippines from 8 December 1941 to 15 June 1942. Personnel who were members of the Bataan or Manila Bay forces, units, ships, or aircraft under enemy attack and stationed in Philippine waters or territories for at least 30 days during this period, were entitled to wear one bronze service star on the ribbon.

Described in all service regulations as a "ribbon," there does not appear to be any regulation-sized medal available to United States personnel. However, miniature medals with metal pendants are readily available for wear with dress uniforms and no objections have been made by the military serv-

161

ices to the wearing of these miniatures. It is not known whether the present government of the Philippines has full-scale medals available for issue. The ribbon is of silk *moiré*, composed of red and white stripes. In the center of the red stripe are three white stars $\frac{1}{8}''$ in circumscribed diameter, with centers placed on extremities of an imaginary equilateral triangle $\frac{1}{4}''$ on each side with one point of each star outward and centered in radiated center lines. The single star is worn uppermost.

Air Force Manual 900-3, Army Regulation 672-5-1, Coast Guard Personnel Manual CG-207, and SECNAVINST 1650.1C are the directives covering this award; established by the Philippine Commonwealth Government by General Order No. 8, Army Headquarters, 1944.

PHILIPPINE LIBERATION RIBBON

Plate 133
(p. 155)

The Philippine Liberation Ribbon was awarded to personnel who participated in the liberation of the Philippines from 17 October 1944 to 3 September 1945. Either combat service or assignment for at least 30 days entitled an individual to the award.

The Philippine Liberation Ribbon is also only a "ribbon," but a miniature metal pendant is available. The award is a silk-*moiré* ribbon of red with equal stripes of blue and white in the center. The blue stripe is worn to the wearer's right. The only devices authorized for wear on the ribbon are bronze service stars.

Air Force Manual 900-3, Army Regulation 672-5-1, Coast Guard Personnel Manual CG-207, and SECNAVINST 1650.1C are the directives covering this award; established by the Philippine Commonwealth Government by General Order No. 8, Army Headquarters, 1944.

PHILIPPINE INDEPENDENCE RIBBON

Plate 134
(p. 155)

The Philippine Independence Ribbon was awarded to personnel who were recipients of the Philippine Defense Ribbon and the Philippine Liberation Ribbon. When first established, it was also awarded to all personnel who were present for duty in Philippine territories or waters on 4 July 1946. In 1954 this latter qualification was deleted from service regulations. However, those who had been awarded the Philippine Independence Ribbon under the earlier criteria were permitted to continue wearing the PIR.

The Philippine Independence Ribbon is also described as a "ribbon" by service regulations and there does not seem to be a miniature medal for wear. The ribbon is predominantly blue, edged with yellow stripes and has, in the center, red, white, and red stripes, in the order named.

Air Force Manual 900-3, Army Regulation 672-5-1, Coast Guard Personnel Manual CG-207, and SECNAVINST 1650.1C are the directives covering this award; established by the Philippine Commonwealth government by General Order No. 383, Army Headquarters, 1946.

UNITED NATIONS SERVICE MEDAL

Plates 135, 136 (p. 156) The United Nations Service Medal was awarded to members of the United States Armed Forces for service in the Korean Theater on behalf of the United Nations Command between 27 June 1950 and 27 July 1954. Personnel who qualified for the Korean Service Medal were usually eligible for this U.N. award.

The medal was made up and issued in the several languages of the U.N. participants in the Korean War. While the obverse of the pendant remained the same, the spelling of "KOREA" on the fixed clasp differed and the words on the reverse "FOR SERVICE IN DEFENSE OF THE PRINCIPLES OF THE CHARTER OF THE UNITED NATIONS" was lettered in the language of the various participating countries. I have also included an illustration of the medal issued to Korean troops.

Designed by a staff of the United Nations, the medal shows British influence in its shape, and is of bright bronze alloy 1.4" in diameter. On the obverse is the emblem of the United Nations. On the reverse is the inscription "FOR SERVICE IN DEFENSE OF THE PRINCIPLES OF THE CHARTER OF THE UNITED NATIONS." The medal is suspended from a silk ribbon 2" long and 1.33" wide consisting of 17 stripes—nine of United Nations blue and eight of white, alternating—each of which is 0.08" wide. A bar 1.5" long and 0.25" wide, bearing the word "KOREA," constitutes a part of the suspension of the medal from the ribbon. There are no devices worn on the ribbon bar or suspension ribbon; however, the metal bar (inscribed with the word "KOREA") is an integral part of the metal pendant.

Air Force Manual 900-3, Army Regulation 672-5-1, Coast Guard Personnel Manual CG-207, and SECNAVINST 1650.1C are the directives covering this award; authorized by United Nations General Assembly Resolution 483(V), 12 December 1950. (Department of Defense Directive 110.23-3, 27 November 1951, authorized its wear by U.S. personnel.)

UNITED NATIONS MEDAL

Plate 137
(p. 156)

The United Nations Medal may be awarded for service with the U.N. Observation Group in Lebanon; the U.N. Truce Supervision Organization in Palestine; the U.N. Military Observation Group in India and Pakistan; and the U.N. Security Forces in Hollandia. Other organizations will be designated as the world situation requires.

The amount of service qualifying an individual for the award will be as designated by the United Nations Secretary General. Individuals who qualify will be awarded the United Nations Medal in the field by the senior representative of the Secretary General.

Designed by the United Nations, the medal is a disk $1\frac{1}{4}''$ in diameter. On the obverse is the emblem of the United Nations and the letters "UN." On the reverse are the words "IN THE SERVICE OF PEACE." The medal is suspended from a ribbon of United Nations blue with two single narrow white stripes $\frac{1}{4}''$ from each edge.

Authority was Secretary General of the United Nations Dispatch 109, 30 July 1959. (Department of Defense Instructions 1348.10, 6 December 1960, promulgated Presidential acceptance for the United States Armed Forces.)

REPUBLIC OF VIETNAM CAMPAIGN MEDAL

Plates 138, 139
(p. 156)

In an unprecedented action, the Department of Defense authorized United States military personnel to accept and wear a service medal tendered by a foreign government. The Vietnam Campaign Medal, a beautifully designed award issued by the government of South Vietnam to its troops, is also awarded to U.S. personnel.

The requirements for award to U.S. servicemen is that they first earn the U.S. Vietnam Service Medal and serve six months in direct support of military operations in Vietnam or in an adjacent country. The military department-decoration regulations do not specify the countries which are providing direct support. If a person is wounded and evacuated before serving a full six months, he also is eligible. Posthumous awards are also made.

There are no provisions to indicate second and subsequent awards. Since the Vietnam government, like several European governments, does not issue service medals, individuals wishing the pendant must purchase it themselves.

The $1\frac{1}{4}''$ medal is gold plated, with two stars, one overlaid on the other, each composed of six points. The points of the above star are white enameled in relief, with gold border. The points of the underneath star are carved in relief, gold plated, with many small brass angles directed toward the center of the medal. In the center is a round frame with a gold border. The inside of the frame is green with the outline of the Vietnamese country in gold plate and a red flame with three rays upright in the center. On the reverse is the inscription "VIETNAM CAMPAIGN MEDAL." The ribbon is edged with green stripes, and alternates green and white stripes, with a white center. A rectangular, silver-plated metal device on the suspension ribbon denotes the period of war, i.e., "1960—." A similar but smaller device with the last two digits of the inclusive years of the war, i.e., "60—," is worn on the ribbon bar. The smaller medal on the right is the size customarily worn with full or mess dress.

Air Force Manual 900-3, Army Regulation 672-5-1, Coast Guard Personnel Manual CG-207, and SECNAVINST 1650.1C are the directives covering this award; authorized by Department of Defense Instructions 1348.17, 20 June 1966, which promulgated Presidential permission to wear the medal.

7

GENERAL RULES
FOR WEARING DECORATIONS AND
SERVICE MEDALS

The precedence and prescribed manner of wear of the various medals, badges, and insignia by members of the United States Armed Forces is complex and would require a separate volume, were one to undertake quoting each service's regulations and directives in detail. Each of our military services issues its own rules on precedence and wear and, while generally similar, no two are exactly alike. On pages 175–79 you will find a listing of the precedence of all the medals issued to members of the various military services as well as directions giving the proper place to wear various awards on the uniform.

There are simple rules for wearing decorations and service medals. Ribbons are usually worn immediately above the left-breast pocket, centered, and most often three to a row. The decorations all have an established rank and are worn with the highest ranking first, the second following in order of importance from the wearer's right to left. Service medals are almost always worn in the order (date) earned. There are exceptions, of course, and those exceptions are covered on pages 175–79. After service medals (U.S.) follow foreign decorations, foreign unit citations, United Nations medals, and foreign service medals.

The services usually permit the individual to decide whether or not to wear his ribbons. All encourage wearing them and on certain occasions will require ribbons as a specific part of the uniform of the day. Ribbons are not worn on work (fatigue) clothing, and cannot be worn on the overcoat. They cannot be worn by prisoners while undergoing punishment imposed by a court-martial.

Ribbons are intended as a convenience to enable a person to display his decorations without wearing the pendant and other devices of the medal. The only time the medals themselves are worn is when the individual is attired in full- or mess-dress uniform, and on special ceremonial occasions.

Miniature replicas of all medals and ribbons, except the Medal of Honor, are usually authorized for wear. Persons wearing the neck ribbon of the Medal of Honor must always display it in full size and wear it suspended around the neck.

All other United States decorations and medals awarded to U.S. personnel are worn on the left breast. When wearing only the ribbon bar of the Medal of Honor, it too is worn on the left breast.

Foreign decorations are always worn following all United States decorations and medals and usually in the order earned. When a person possesses more than one decoration from the same country, the decorations are worn in the manner prescribed by that nation. When attending affairs at which a specific nation is the host or guest of honor, the awards a person receives from that country are worn before all other foreign decorations as a courtesy. Foreign awards may not be worn on the United States uniform unless at least one U.S. award is displayed.

The Army wears all U.S. unit awards above the right pocket. Members of the Air Force, Navy, Marine Corps, and Coast Guard wear the unit award emblems in a size reduced to that of service ribbons and sandwiched in with their other ribbons. When worn with other ribbons, unit awards follow decorations and precede service medals.

The emblems of the Philippine Presidential Unit Citation, the Korean Presidential Unit Citation, and Vietnam Presidential Unit Citation, when worn by Army personnel, are worn above the right pocket, following U.S. unit awards.

The Air Force, Navy, Marine Corps, and Coast Guard wear foreign presidential unit citations with their ribbons following foreign decorations and preceding the United Nations Service Medal or other foreign service medals, such as the Republic of Vietnam Campaign Medal.

The Korean citation is worn with the red part of the *taeguk* (circle) uppermost. The Philippine citation is worn with the blue section on the wearer's right.

Other foreign unit awards worn by U.S. personnel include the fourragères of the French Croix de Guerre and Medaille

Militaire; the Citation in the Order of the Day of the Belgian Army; and the Netherlands Lanyard. These are always worn looped through the left epaulet.

Generally ribbons will be worn in this way: personal U.S. military decorations first, followed by nonmilitary U.S. government agency decorations, U.S. unit awards (ribbon type), Combat Readiness Medal, Good Conduct medals, U.S. service and campaign medals, Philippine decorations and medals, foreign decorations and unit awards (ribbon type), United Nations medals, and, finally, foreign service and campaign medals.

No ribbons, decorations, badges, or insignia issued by any organization or agency subordinate to the United States government may be worn on the uniform of members of the armed forces. Members of the reserve forces, including the National Guard, may wear state-awarded ribbons on the uniform, but must remove these nonfederal awards when they are called to extended, federally recognized active duty. No nonmilitary U.S. government decorations may be worn on the uniform unless U.S. military decorations or service medals are worn.

When in full- or mess-dress uniform, miniature replicas of pendant-type medals are ordinarily the only size worn. Exceptions to this are the Medal of Honor and foreign neck, sash, or sunburst decorations or orders. No more than one neck, one sash and/or one sunburst-type foreign decoration will be worn at one time. When a person wears both a neck-type foreign decoration, and a Medal of Honor, the Medal of Honor is always placed atop the foreign decoration. Qualification badges and unit citations are not worn on the full- or mess-dress uniform.

Qualification badges are usually worn on the left breast above any ribbons. Exceptions to this are Army and Marine Corps marksmanship badges, driver qualification badges and, when a person has both the Combat Infantryman's Badge and Parachutist's Badge, the latter will be worn on the pocket flap below ribbons.

8

APPURTENANCES AND DEVICES
TO MEDALS AND RIBBONS

Appurtenances and devices to ribbons are a means of recognizing additional awards for or to the basic medal or ribbon. Laws of the United States preclude the award of more than one particular medal to an individual.

In order to recognize the achievements and services of persons who may have been awarded more than one of the same decorations, and those who have performed unusual or distinctive actions or services, certain devices are awarded to be worn on the ribbon bar and suspension ribbon to denote that service or subsequent award.

The following list of appurtenances and devices to awards and decorations is as complete as possible as of date of publication.

WEAR OF APPURTENANCES ON DECORATIONS AND SERVICE AWARDS

OAK LEAF CLUSTERS: When an Oak Leaf Cluster is worn on a decoration, it will be centered on the ribbon. When two or more are worn, they are arranged an equal distance apart from the ends of the ribbon and are centered as much as possible. When both a silver and a bronze oak-leaf cluster are worn, the silver will be to the wearer's right.

BRONZE, SILVER, AND GOLD CLASPS TO THE ARMY GOOD CONDUCT MEDAL: Only one color of clasp may be worn on the Army Good Conduct Medal. It is centered on the ribbon.

BRONZE AND SILVER STARS $(\frac{3}{16}'')$: When a $\frac{3}{16}''$ star is worn on a ribbon, it will be centered on the ribbon. When two or more are worn they are arranged an equal distance apart from the end of the ribbon and centered as much as possible. When both a silver and a bronze star are worn, the silver star will be to the wearer's right.

SILVER AND GOLD STARS $(\frac{5}{16}'')$: When a $\frac{5}{16}''$ star is worn on a ribbon, it will be centered. When two or more are worn they are arranged an equal distance apart from the ends of the ribbon and centered as much as possible. When both a gold and a silver star are worn, the silver will be to the wearer's right.

BRONZE V DEVICE: When a bronze V device is worn, it will be centered on the ribbon. When another device (oak-leaf cluster or star) is worn, the two devices are arranged an equal distance apart from the ends of the ribbon and centered as much as possible with the V device always worn to the right of the ribbon.

HOUR GLASS DEVICE: The Hour Glass Device is worn centered on the Armed Forces Reserve Medal only. When two or more are worn, they are arranged an equal distance apart from the ends of the ribbon and centered as much as possible.

SILVER LETTER W: When the Silver Letter W is worn on the Navy Expeditionary Medal, it is placed in the center of the ribbon.

BRONZE LETTER A: When the Bronze Letter A is worn on the American Defense Service Medal, it is placed in the center of the ribbon. When wearing the A device, no star can be worn on the ribbon.

FLEET MARINE FORCE COMBAT OPERATION INSIGNIA: When this insignia is worn on the ribbon, it is centered and battle stars are placed alternately, the first to the right of the insignia, the second to the left, etc.

BRONZE MALTESE CROSS: The Bronze Maltese Cross is worn centered on the World War I Victory Medal.

GERMANY AND JAPAN CLASPS: Either or both clasps may be worn on the suspension ribbon of the Army of Occupation Medal, but may not be worn on the ribbon bar.

ASIA AND EUROPE CLASPS: Either or both clasps may be worn on the suspension ribbon of the Navy Occupation Service Medal, but may not be worn on the ribbon bar.

FLEET, BASE, OR FOREIGN SERVICE CLASPS: These may be worn on the suspension ribbon only of the American Defense Service Medal. A bronze $\frac{3}{16}''$ star is worn on the ribbon bar to denote possession of the clasp.

WAKE ISLAND CLASP: The Wake Island Clasp is worn on the Navy Expeditionary Medal suspension ribbon only. A silver letter W indicates possession of the clasp on the ribbon bar.

BRONZE ARROWHEADS: Bronze Arrowheads may be worn on the suspension ribbon and the ribbon bar. They are placed to the right of all other devices on the ribbon.

BERLIN AIRLIFT DEVICE: The Berlin Airlift Device may be worn with both the suspension ribbon and ribbon bar of the Army of Occupation Medal or Navy Occupation Service Medal. When wearing the Berlin Airlift Device, the nose of the aircraft device is pointed at a 30-degree angle toward the wearer's right shoulder.

AN INSCRIBED BRONZE BAR may be worn on the Specially Meritorious Medal suspension ribbon to indicate a second award of the medal.

AN INSCRIBED BRONZE BAR may be worn on the suspension ribbon of the Haitian Campaign Medal to indicate the wearer served in both Haitian campaigns.

BRONZE SERVICE, DEFENSIVE SECTOR, AND BATTLE CLASPS may be worn only on the suspension ribbon of the World War I Victory Medal.

ARABIC NUMERALS: Arabic numerals may be worn on the ribbon bar and suspension ribbon of the Air Medal by Navy and Marine Corps personnel.

BRONZE GLOBE: Worn on the Navy Presidential Unit Citation ribbon by personnel of the U.S.S. *Triton* who were aboard the ship when it was cited.

GOLD N: Worn on the Navy Presidential Unit Citation ribbon by personnel of the U.S.S. *Nautilus* who were aboard the ship when it was cited.

WINTERED-OVER CLASP: Worn on the Antartica Service Medal suspension ribbon to show that a person remained on the Antarctic continent through a winter. In bronze, gold, and silver for wintering over for one, two, or three winters respectively.

WINTERED-OVER DISK: Worn on the ribbon bar of the Antarctica Service Medal in the same manner as the WINTERED-OVER CLASP.

APPENDIX

1. PRECEDENCE OF AWARDS

WHEN WORN BY AIR FORCE PERSONNEL

Medal of Honor
Air Force Cross[1]
Distinguished Service Medal[1]
Silver Star
Legion of Merit
Distinguished Flying Cross
Airman's Medal[1]
Bronze Star Medal
Meritorious Service Medal
Air Medal
Joint Service Commendation Medal
Air Force Commendation Medal[1]
Purple Heart
Presidential Unit Citation[1]
Air Force Outstanding Unit Award[1]
U.S. Nonmilitary Decorations[2]
Combat Readiness Medal
Good Conduct Medal[1]
American Defense Service Medal
Women's Army Corps Service Medal
American Campaign Medal[3]

Asiatic Pacific Campaign Medal[3]
European-African-Middle Eastern Campaign Medal[3]
World War II Victory Medal
Army of Occupation Medal[3]
Medal for Humane Action
National Defense Service Medal[3]
Korean Service Medal[3]
Antarctica Service Medal[3]
Armed Forces Expeditionary Medal[3]
Vietnam Service Medal[3]
National Defense Service Medal (2nd)[3]
Air Force Longevity Service Award
Armed Forces Reserve Medal
Air Reserve Forces Meritorious Service Ribbon
Noncommissioned Officer Academy Graduate Ribbon
Small Arms Expert Marksmanship Ribbon
Philippine Defense Ribbon

Philippine Liberation Ribbon
Philippine Independence
Ribbon
Merchant Marine Combat
Bar
Merchant Marine War Zone
Bars
Foreign Decorations
Philippine Presidential Unit
Citation

Republic of Korea Presiden-
tial Unit Citation
Other Foreign Unit Citations
United Nations Service
Medal
United Nations Medal
Foreign Service Medals

1 The Navy Cross and Army Distinguished Service medals have
comparable rank, but are worn on the Air Force uniform following the
Air Force Cross, in order earned. The same applies to other medals
marked "1".
2 Nonmilitary U.S. decorations are worn by rank, but generally
between the gold and silver lifesaving medals if both are possessed by
wearer.
3 Worn in order earned.

WHEN WORN BY ARMY PERSONNEL

Medal of Honor
Distinguished Service Cross[1]
Distinguished Service Medal[1]
Silver Star
Legion of Merit
Distinguished Flying Cross
Soldier's Medal[1]
Bronze Star Medal
Meritorious Service Medal
Air Medal
Joint Service Commendation
Medal
Army Commendation
Medal[1]
Purple Heart
U.S. Nonmilitary Decora-
tions[2]
Merchant Marine Decora-
tions
Good Conduct Medal[1]
American Defense Service
Medal

Women's Army Corps Serv-
ice Medal
American Campaign Medal[3]
Asiatic Pacific Campaign
Medal[3]
European-African-Middle
Eastern Campaign Medal[3]
World War II Victory Medal
Army of Occupation Medal
Medal for Humane Action
National Defense Service
Medal
Korean Service Medal
Antarctica Service Medal[3]
Armed Forces Expeditionary
Medal[3]
Vietnam Service Medal[3]
National Defense Service
Medal (2nd)[3]
Armed Forces Reserve Medal
Philippine Defense Ribbon
Philippine Liberation Ribbon

Philippine Independence
Ribbon
Merchant Marine Combat
Bar

Merchant Marine War Zone
Bars
Foreign Decorations
Foreign Service Medals

Army personnel wear all Unit Citations on their right breast. Precedence of these is:

Presidential Unit Citation
(Army)
Presidential Unit Citation
(Navy)
Valorous Unit Emblem

Meritorious Unit Emblem
Navy Unit Commendation
Air Force Outstanding Unit
Award
Foreign Unit Awards

1 Other branches of the service have awards that rank equally, but holders of more than one of equally ranked ribbons wear the ribbon of their parent service first, with others following in order earned.

2 Nonmilitary U.S. decorations are worn by rank, but generally between the gold and silver lifesaving medals if both are possessed by wearer.

3 Worn in order earned.

WHEN WORN BY NAVY, MARINE CORPS & COAST GUARD PERSONNEL

Medal of Honor
Navy Cross[1]
Distinguished Service Medal[1]
Silver Star
Legion of Merit
Distinguished Flying Cross
Navy and Marine Corps
Medal[1]
Bronze Star Medal
Meritorious Service Medal
Air Medal
Joint Service Commendation
Medal
Commendation Medal[1]
Navy Achievement Medal
Purple Heart
Presidential Unit Citation[1]
Navy Unit Commendation
Meritorious Unit Commendation

Good Conduct Medal[1]
Navy Reserve Medal
Navy Reserve Meritorious
Service Medal
Organized Marine Corps
Reserve Medal
Byrd Antarctic Expedition
Medal
Second Byrd Antarctic Expedition Medal
U.S. Antarctic Expedition
Medal
Expeditionary Medal, Navy
or Marine Corps[2]
Victory Medal, World
War I[2]
Haitian Campaign Medal
(1919–20)[2]
Second Nicaraguan Campaign Medal[2]

Yangtze Service Medal[2]
China Service Medal[2]
American Defense Service
  Medal[2]
American Campaign Medal
European-African-Middle
  Eastern Campaign Medal[2]
Asiatic-Pacific Campaign
  Medal[2]
Victory Medal, World
  War II
Medal For Humane Action[2]
Navy Occupation Service
  Medal[2]
National Defense Service
  Medal[2]
Korean Service Medal[2]
Antarctic Service Medal
Armed Forces Expeditionary
  Medal[2]
Vietnam Service Medal[2]

Armed Forces Reserve Medal
Marine Corps Reserve
  Ribbon
Foreign Decorations
United Nations Service
  Medal
United Nations Medal
Philippine Defense Ribbon
Philippine Liberation Ribbon
Philippine Independence
  Ribbon
Philippine Republic Presi-
  dential Unit Citation
Republic of Korea Presiden-
  tial Unit Citation
Republic of Vietnam Presi-
  dential Unit Citation
Republic of Vietnam Cam-
  paign Medal
Marksmanship Awards

1 Other branches of the service have awards that rank equally, but holders of more than one of equally ranked ribbons wear the ribbon of their parent service first, with others following in order earned.
2 Worn in order earned.

PRECEDENCE OF AWARDS
AND DECORATIONS
THAT ARE NOW OBSOLETE

ARMY
Certificate of Merit
Civil War Medal
Indian Campaign Medal
Spanish Campaign Medal
Spanish War Service Medal
Army of Cuba Occupation
  Medal
Army of Puerto Rico Occu-
  pation Medal
Philippine Campaign Medal

NAVY
Marine Corps Brevet Medal
Specially Meritorious Medal
Dewey Medal
Sampson Medal
Peary Polar Expedition
  Medal
NC-4 Medal
Civil War Medal
West Indies Naval Campaign
  Medal

ARMY	*NAVY*
China Campaign Medal	China Relief Expedition Medal
Philippine Congressional Medal	Philippine Campaign Medal
Army of Cuba Pacification Medal	West Indies Campaign Medal
Mexican Service Medal	Spanish Campaign Medal
Mexican Border Service Medal	Navy Cuban Pacification Medal
Victory Medal, World War I	Peary Polar Expedition Medal
Occupation of Germany Medal (WWI)	Nicaraguan Campaign Medal
	Haitian Campaign Medal
	Dominican Campaign Medal
	Mexican Service Medal
	Victory Medal, World War I

2. HOW TO APPLY FOR EARNED MEDALS

Most men who left the service at the end of World War II and the Korean War were never issued the medals to which they were entitled. The mass exodus made it physically impossible to stock all these awards, and in many cases, the actual medals themselves were not yet designed. Others in their anxiety to finish their military service, simply did not want to be bothered.

If one should wish to obtain the medals and awards which he earned in the service, but was never issued, he can obtain them by writing to the appropriate address. In your letter, provide your full name, service rank, service (serial) number (all of them if more than one), and dates of active military service. If you still have a military status, i.e., retired or reservist, check with the Personnel Office at the nearest installation of your service. There are different rules in this case.

EX-NAVY PERSONNEL: Chief of Naval Personnel
                                    Department of the Navy
                                    Washington, D.C. 20370

EX-AIR FORCE PERSONNEL: Commander
                                    NPRC (MPR-AF)
                                    9700 Page Boulevard
                                    St Louis, Missouri 63132

EX-MARINE PERSONNEL: Commandant
                                    US Marine Corps
                                    Washington, D.C. 20380

EX-COAST GUARD PERSONNEL: Commandant
                                    US Coast Guard
                                    13th & E Streets, NW
                                    Washington, D.C. 20226

EX-ARMY PERSONNEL: Commanding Officer
                                    US Army Administration
                                       Center
                                    9700 Page Boulevard
                                    St Louis, Missouri 63132

BIBLIOGRAPHY

Air Force Manual 900-3, *Decorations, Service Awards, Unit Awards, Special Badges, Favorable Communications, Certificates and Special Devices,* U.S. Government Printing Office, Washington, 1966

Air Force Regulation 900-7, *Decorations,* U.S. Government Printing Office, Washington, 1953

Air Force Regulation 900-10, *Service Awards,* U.S. Government Printing Office, Washington, 1961

Air Force Regulation 35-50, *Service Awards, Medals, Ribbons and Devices,* U.S. Government Printing Office, Washington, 1953

Air Force Regulation 35-75, *Unit Awards,* U.S. Government Printing Office, Washington, 1954

Air Force Manual 35-10, *Service and Dress Uniforms for Air Force Personnel,* U.S. Government Printing Office, Washington, 1968

Air Force General Order 60, Department of the Air Force, Washington, 1957

Army Regulations 672-5-1, *Awards,* U.S. Government Printing Office, Washington, 1961, 1962, 1963, 1965, 1966

Army Regulation 672-5-2, *Decorations and Awards, Illustrations of Awards,* U.S. Government Printing Office, Washington, 1967

Army Information Digest, U.S. Government Printing Office, Washington, September, 1963

American Badges and Insignia, Evans E. Kerrigan, Viking Press, New York, 1967

American War Medals and Decorations, Evans E. Kerrigan, Viking Press, New York, 1964

Department of Transportation Order DOT 3400.1 Order, 27 July 1967

Insignia and Decorations of the United States Armed Forces,

National Geographic Society, Washington, 1 December 1944

Heroes, United States Marine Corps, 1861–1955, Jane Blakeney, Marine Corps Association, Washington, 1957

Medal of Honor 1863–1968, prepared for Committee on Labor and Public Welfare, 90th Congress. U.S. Government Printing Office, Washington, 1968

Medal of Honor of the United States Army, Government Printing Office, Washington, 1948

Medal of Honor of the United States Navy, 1861–1948, U.S. Government Printing Office, Washington, 1949

Military Medals and Insignia of the United States, J. McDowell Morgan, Griffin-Patterson Glendale, California, 1941

Navy and Marine Corps Awards Manual, Department of the Navy, Bureau of Personnel, NAVPERS 15,790, Government Printing Office, Washington, 1953

Navy Personnel Instruction P1650.1C Department of the Navy, Bureau of Personnel, U.S. Government Printing Office, Washington, 1963

Orders, Decorations and Insignia, Military and Civil, Colonel Robert E. Wyllie, Putnam, New York, 1927

Ribbons & Meaais, Naval, Military, Air Force and Civil, Captain H. Taprell Dorling, London, George Philip & Son Ltd., Editions of 1956, 1957, 1960, and 1963

United States War Medals, Belden, Bauman L. American Numismatic Society, Washington, 1915

INDEX OF MEDALS AND RIBBONS